031104

P9-BYC-854

M

U 25 JUL 1977

2 MAR 1988

Rudolph Valentino

Other books by Alexander Walker
The Celluloid Sacrifice
Stardom
Stanley Kubrick Directs
Hollywood England

B
VAL
1

RUDOLPH
VALENTINO

by
Alexander Walker

SHOALHAVEN SHIRE LIBRARY ★

ELM TREE BOOKS/
HAMISH HAMILTON LONDON

for Andrew Grima, another perfectionist

First published in Great Britain, 1976
by Elm Tree Books/Hamish Hamilton Ltd
90 Great Russell Street London WC1B 3PT
Copyright © 1976, Alexander Walker
SBN 241 89349 6

Designed by Lawrence Edwards
Filmset by BAS Printers Limited Wallop Hampshire
Printed by Ebenezer Baylis, Worcester

Acknowledgements

THE AUTHOR AND publishers wish to express their special thanks to Leslie Flint, President of the Valentino Memorial Guild, for his advice and assistance in assembling many of the illustrations used in this book. They also thank Norman A. Mackenzie and Mrs Russell E. Dill for permission to reproduce the photographs on pages 12 and 13, Richard Buckle for help in locating the photograph on page 52, the National Film Archive Stills library, and Associated Press.

Every effort has been made to trace the copyright holders of the photographic material used in this volume. Should there be any omissions in this respect, we apologise and shall be pleased to make the appropriate acknowledgement in future editions.

1

THE 'GREAT LOVER' is a name that has fallen into disuse without ever quite losing its fascination for us. The man who has power over women today is called a 'male chauvinist' if he ever dares exert his power; not so very long ago he would have been merely called a 'playboy', but already that name has gathered its own quaint sense of anachronism in a world of scarcity. In any case, both 'male chauvinist' and 'playboy' are words that provide us with information about the prevailing attitudes of sexual permissiveness at one time or another, whereas the attribute of being a 'Great Lover' concentrates our curiosity and possibly even our envy on the man himself, the title-holder in question. In the 1920s that man was pre-eminently Rudolph Valentino.

Despite that celebrated habit of The Sheik's, of abducting young, unaccompanied ladies in the desert and forcing his attentions on them in his tent, Valentino is not be perfunctorily categorised as a 'male chauvinist'. Indeed his own sex frequently regarded him with suspicion and, at times, with downright derision. Nor was he an off-screen 'playboy'. His life is oddly devoid of the compulsive promiscuity or lurid scandal to which other stars fell victim, when they did not actively seek it. There are other paradoxes, too. His career lasted barely seven years on the screen, yet the magnetic appeal he possessed for women the world over has outlasted his premature death, aged only thirty-one, so that along with his countryman, Casanova, his name is virtually a synonym for tireless ardour in the pursuit and capture of women. Furthermore, he projected his ardour without speech, or at least without being heard to speak, for he died in 1926, just before the talkies could have carried his voice to the devoted millions who knew only his mute, luminous presence on the silent screen. Then, again, the Valentino cult took root—*instant* root—at a time when women in general, and American women in particular, were far from predisposed to submit themselves to any man's bondage. The years immediately after the First World War, and most of the 1920s, was a period when women went about conspicuously asserting the right to their own enjoyment of life. Not quite Women's Lib, but rather more fun. The range of personal pleasures and permitted public experiences widened dramatically once women on war work had loosened the corset of old social constraints and then found that peacetime prosperity gave their purses the jingle of independence. To be borne away at such a time supine across an Arabian saddle, or jacknifed willy-nilly into a sensuous tango by an Argentine gaucho, in short to be there for the taking by a man so supremely confident of his claims over you—it was a perverse way of celebrating your sex's emancipation.

Such enigmas as these are what make Valentino an object of abiding contemporary speculation. Of all the great silent film stars, Pickford, Fairbanks, Gish, Chaplin, Gilbert, Swanson, yes, even Garbo who has had her mystery diluted if not quite dispersed by one of her intimate friends who has recently turned tale-teller, Valentino is the personality who keeps us guessing. A large part of such guess-work, it must be conceded, is about his own sexual nature. He was a 'Great Lover', all right, but was he a *potent* one, too? In his lifetime he had to suffer sly innuendoes and sometimes frankly libellous sneers of disbelief directed at his masculinity, which were a source of grief to him and, some said, a contributory cause of his death. That tendency is, if anything, even stronger nowadays. We aren't a bit surprised in this sceptical age if our public idols have feet of clay and in the case of a man renowned for his sex appeal that even more intimate parts of him could prove weak if put to the test. Largely because both of his marriages were as far as we know unconsummated, it's been concluded that Valentino must have been impotent. And since he had a lifelong attraction to women who were stronger-willed than himself, and scornful of sex even though they worked in an industry reputed to be oversexed, it's been alleged that he was homosexual. Such speculations require investigation. But they shouldn't blind us to the fact that Valentino's own sexual identity, on screen and off it, is a more complex affair than gossipy insinuation allows.

What all such paradoxes add up to is the mystery of how and why this particular man at one particular time became a world-wide star and an object of fascination to millions who would never feel his embrace or his kisses. 'Who are you, my lord? I do not know your name,' asks the dancing girl of the sheik she has met in the moonlight by the temple in Valentino's last film. 'I am he that loves you,' comes the confident answer. 'Is not that enough?' In days of simpler faith, no doubt it was. Nowadays, with unbelievers present, we require a little more explanation.

2

IN ONE OF his films, as Monsieur Beaucaire, a French nobleman disguised as a barber, he raises his arms when he's been unmasked and ironically 'conducts' the man reading out his flamboyant titles as if they were a concerto being played by a symphony orchestra. The flowery string of names bestowed on Valentino at birth usually incites the same gentle mockery. In fact they are as documentary as any parish register. They reveal the descent that fused into his later character. From his father Giovanni Guglielmi, an ex-cavalry captain turned veterinary surgeon, he got the names 'Rodolpho Alfonzo Raffaelo'; from his mother, a French surgeon's daughter, he inherited the 'Pierre Filibert'; and the cognomen 'di Valentina d'Antonguolla' combined an old Papal title with a claim the Guglielmis still asserted to certain estates they had forfeited near Martina Franca where they originally came from, though Valentino was born, on 6 May 1895, in the nearby inland town of Castellaneta, just under Italy's 'heel'. With this ancestry, it's no surprise that he was bilingual from an early age. It's French he actually speaks, even if he's not *heard* speaking it, throughout much of *Monsieur Beaucaire*, according to lip-readers anyhow, obviously in order to 'assume' the character more completely. Like many boys from Southern Italy who go into the hotel and restaurant trade, Valentino had a facility for languages. The memoirs of his second wife, Natacha Rambova, refer to his 'entering into the actualities of the Spanish character'—the bullfighter in *Blood and Sand*—'and speaking Spanish so perfectly, without the slightest accent, that he was continually taken for a real Spaniard.'

English, too, he learned early, and vernacularly, when he came to America. Not one interviewer in all the years he was a star refers to Valentino's having the slightest language difficulty. Rambova says he retained 'a slight foreign accent'. To those who remember it, this accent was not markedly Italian: it had, if anything, a French flavour. It's worth stressing this early on to give the lie to doubters who believe the onset of the talkies would have finished Valentino as a screen actor. The likelihood is that his vocal fluency, his 'romantic' accent, would have carried him safely into the sound era, perhaps even

9

Valentino (left) in his mid-teens photographed with a companion in the uniform of the agricultural college he attended before going to America

increased his appeal as it did Greta Garbo's, though obviously his exoticism would have had to adapt to the greater realism of speaking parts.

He doesn't seem to have had any strong religious conviction from his upbringing: which was just as well considering that his two marriages, contracted in civil courts, ended in divorce. His father's early death encouraged his indiscipline: his school records speak of inattentiveness except at gymnastics and dancing-classes. Future film stars could have had worse kindergartens than the gym-hall and dance-floor. Most of the other evidence about Valentino's adolescence is either lost or in doubt, being heavily 'retouched' by hindsight or thoroughly fabricated by fan magazines after he had achieved stardom. But the earliest photograph of the Valentino the world knew may be a snapshot taken with two young American ladies aboard the *S.S. Cleveland* on which he was sailing to America in December 1913, after his mother had (thankfully, one supposes) yielded to his entreaties to be allowed to try his luck in a land where the generation just before his had become the newest of the immigrant waves and was sending home news about work or prospects. These snapshots, which are in a private collection, show a young Valentino, aged eighteen which effectively kills the legend of the poor immigrant boy wearing sheets of newspaper under his shirt to keep out the cold. A smart young masher is the word for him, already self-composed and elegantly got-up, sporting a jaunty Jackie Coogan-like cap, with the 'V' of a white vest peeping from under a jacket which the wind on deck is whipping in close to the suggestion of a neat waist. The supple physique is already there: so, incidentally, are the women whom Valentino and another Italian youth are keeping amused by their camera antics.

So, too, are qualities that the movie camera would record with uncommon sympathy, those of pose and repose. They are the qualities that make a good dancer and—so thought the film director Rex Ingram—'a good screen actor'. The 'Great Lover' has found *his* first lover—the camera.

If such qualities were inherent in him, Valentino found that life in America swiftly brought them into use. He is said to have taken a job as a gardener's boy on a Long Island estate, where one imaginative biographer has him apeing and absorbing the manners of the rich at long distance. The greater likelihood is that he learned the essentials of being Valentino from women, and at close range, in the bars and cafés of New York City. It must have been fascinating to him to find how 'approachable' young girls were in America compared to their Southern Italian sisters. And if the 'ghetto' life of Little Italy fraternised easily with native Americans it was in the flux of the dance-floor where physical proximity removed the barrier of ethnic difficulties. American girls were coming singly or in pairs to the *thé-dansants* where 'taxi-dancers', well-groomed and impecunious young men, would partner them round the floor for a discreet fee and provide a sensation of playful flirtatiousness, at least while the music lasted. Amidst the small-talk of the dance-floor, Valentino could perfect his English, and something else far more useful in the silent movies—the ways of making himself agreeable to an ever-changing female clientele. Naturally gregarious, he found himself drifting into regular employment in the dance halls, playing a role, taking part in the understanding 'masquerade' with a woman before any camera was around to record it. There were drawbacks of course. Partnering

Two of the most remarkable photos of Valentino, which have only recently come to light. They were taken aboard the S.S.Cleveland in December, 1913, during the then unknown Rodolpho's voyage to America and they show him (in a jaunty cap) and another male companion with two American ladies, Miss Marion G. Hennion and Miss Eleanor Post (later Mrs Russell E. Dill). The ladies were reputed to have taught Valentino the dance steps of the tango during the voyage: they remained in touch with him during his early months in New York and he escorted them to fashionable parties. Even then he impressed people by the personality and good manners that later contributed so much to his appeal

women gave him a commanding ease with them, but a very incomplete kind of satisfaction. The less than flattering insights he had into the sex as a whole can't have turned him into an overnight romantic. What he did, he did for pay and couldn't be choosy about his clients. There is an analogy here, surely, with the young Greta Garbo whose work at lathering men's chins in a backstreet Stockholm barber's enforced a tolerance of men in their less appetising moments which she later converted into that laconic knowledge of the sex which informs her femininity on the screen—and her chillier reserve off it. Though Valentino never wanted 'to be alone', as people believed Garbo did, he must have felt at times that being at the beck and call of women had the undertones of a gigolo. This cheap stereotype of the Italian Casanova, the seducer battening on women for what they were worth in sex and cash, was something he always bridled over. It even made him refuse (or at least think twice about) the 'bit' parts he was offered in his early movies; for an Italian character on the screen at this date was synonymous with a heartless scoundrel who left a woman irretrievably compromised.

There is an early photograph of Valentino at this period, showing him togged up in a conspicuously 'smart' outfit: it is just the sort of

The importance of appearance: Valentino in rented finery poses for a New York photographer. The photograph is dated 1915 and inscribed to his brother and sister back in Italy

studio portrait that thousands of Italian boys like him had taken to send back home as evidence of how well they were doing in the New World. As a basic defence against the reality of the hand-to-mouth life he was leading, it retains a pathos that the self-conscious life-style of film stardom lacks, even though both images are part of the same illusion. The line between knowing who you were and what you posed as was blurred early; and perhaps Valentino's sexual identity was even at this stage being influenced by the fact that the source of one's power over women was lodged in the illusion of one's trade and not necessarily in the traits of one's personality.

It came as a relief when his dancing proficiency gained him an introduction to Bonnie Glass. She was in search of a partner to replace Clifton Webb in their exhibition performances, at Maxim's or Delmonico's, to the music of the maxixe, the one-step and the tango. The tango had been imported from Latin America: its languorous rhythms supposedly derived from the gauchos dragging their spurred boots over the thick carpets of the brothels. Rodolpho di Valentina, as he now called himself, was helped in suggesting its ethnic eroticism by his own dark, Latin looks. At this time, 1915–1916, the twenty-year-old dancer was wearing a corset under his evening clothes, which at least suggests he was eating well. He put on weight easily and had to watch his diet all through his career. But it was his wrist-watch, then a novelty amongst a man's wardrobe, which was considered a rather more effeminate accoutrement than a posture belt. These facts we know because they were quoted in a derisory tone by the assistant D.A. who led a police raid on a New York apartment house in September 1916, after receiving complaints of blackmail and extortion. Among those arrested on the premises was 'a handsome fellow' named Rodolpho Guglielmi who called himself 'a marquis'. (This was not quite Valentino's first appearance in the papers outside the review columns of the dancing acts. Some weeks earlier he had been a witness against a former dancing partner, one Joan Sawyer, in a divorce suit that the New York socialite Bianca De Saulles was bringing against her husband.)

The police file on Valentino's arrest in the apartment house has long

since disappeared. Getting such awkward evidence out of the way was a fairly common practice when the Hollywood studios had a heavy investment tied up in some star and didn't wish to see old and possibly damaging scandals surfacing again. But the *New York Times* still carries the report, as the biographer Irving Shulman discovered. Apparently print wasn't so permeable to influence as the police blotter. Some believe Valentino was utterly innocent, just a well-meaning dupe who happened to be caught on the spot, others think he had seen a quick way to easy money through the loose living and lavish spending of the night-club set on whom he used his charm when they met professionally. There is no telling which is true; but apparently he was a minor figure in the case, for the graft charge was dropped and he was turned loose after a few days in The Tombs prison. All the same, an immigrant who attracted a charge like that put himself in jeopardy of a deportation order.

When Bianca De Saulles next made headline news on a charge of killing her husband, Valentino prudently fled New York in case he was once again compromised by the company he had kept. He travelled across America in the cast of a touring musical, then moved on to Los Angeles to live on his skill as a dancer in the night-clubs and to try to pick up 'bit' parts in movies. He had arrived, geographically at least, in Hollywood.

3

THERE WAS ALREADY an essentially actorish mix in Valentino's pre-movie personality. We can conclude that he found the environment much more to his taste than even New York's show-business side: for one thing, it was more comfortable to be out of work in the sunshine of California. He made himself *simpatico* with everyone, for this was part of his nature as well as a necessary side of the life he led. There were always Italian mechanics at the local garage who let him 'borrow' a car to impress a potential employer, or simply slide underneath one of the custom-built automobiles and just tinker—he was a born tinkerer, a gadget-lover, a novelty seeker, able to immerse himself easily and contentedly in anything that caught his fancy. This was useful training for the demands of stardom. Another aspect emerged in these early days. He was never without friends, though invariably they were male cronies and generally bachelors, whose names crop up throughout the brief but sensational years of his career when they formed his 'court circle' and provided him with amusement, companionship and distraction from the stern ideals that his second wife was to inculcate into him. For a trouble-free life, one in which he was simply *himself* and not a 'Great Lover', it was safer to Valentino's way of thinking to relax with buddies than flirt with girls.

He first appeared in films as a 'dress extra' in a ballroom scene in *Alimony* in 1917, and the next year he had similar 'bit' parts, playing in swift, forgettable sequence an Italian tough-guy, a medieval knight in armour, even an Irishman, until he landed his first role as a leading man: a socialite's son in *A Society Sensation* in 1918. Anyone knowing the career that was to come feels distinctly uncomfortable watching this film. It is hardly the future style of the 'Great Lover' to be saved from drowning by the leading lady (Carmel Myers) when he gets cramp. And what is even worse, he loses his nerve proposing to the girl. Where he holds his own is sartorially. His trim, dandyish figure reveals the professional dancer, accustomed to carrying his clothes, not being oppressed by them. Valentino's physique is instantly and attractively noticeable: he used it almost in compensation for having to play a wretched succession of 'society' villains over the next year, 'Latin ladykillers' and 'cabaret parasites', which grated on his Italian

Before the days of stardom: Mae Murray got him the small part of a European count in her 1919 film The Delicious Little Devil— *but he had to take a cut in pay to $100 a week*

sensitivities. He is very light on his toes. He can gesture a girl into his private apartments as if preparing to partner her in a dance, not seduce her. When he kisses a girl in the rose bushes, he bears down on her, tango-fashion, as if both of them were going to finish up prostrate on the earth, then retrieves her at the last second by using his body as a counterweight. One reviewer even underlined Valentino's bearing and grooming by remarking how out of character it was for an American (*sic*) actor to look so immaculate—a hint of just one of the things that a few years later had the American males in full cry after Valentino.

He was in and out of nearly a dozen cheaply budgeted, quickly made films and danced with Carol Dempster on the stage in the prologue to a film directed by D. W. Griffith, who didn't divine his romantic appeal, before he was cast for the picture that profoundly influenced his future. This was *Eyes of Youth*, a society melodrama directed by Albert Parker and released in 1919. The star was Clara Kimball Young and Valentino played the kind of part he detested, a professional co-respondent with a fur-collared coat, curly-brimmed bowler and a rather vulgar walk. But once the compromising seduction gets under way in a roadhouse, Valentino's movements have an amorous delicacy quite unlike any American film actor of the period. His poise and methodical intentions, the way he confidently pours himself a drink, helps the lady off with her shawl and stifles her cry for help with single-minded suppleness all show him to be master of the intimate situation. There is a deference about his villainy: his 'Latin-ness' actually lightens the character, adding an element of sexual appeal to its mercenary basis. Valentino appeared in only one reel of *Eyes of Youth*, but the impression he made was enough to win him the part that made him instantly famous, that of Julio the playboy in *The Four Horsemen of the Apocalypse*.

From this point on, Valentino's career reflects the firm foothold that several exceptionally determined and creative women had established for themselves and their sex in the early, prolific youth of Hollywood—and only one of these was a film star. June Mathis was a writer and one of the most highly regarded in the business, a specialist in adapting literary works for the screen. She had headed the Metro and Goldwyn script departments and her advice on the directing and casting of films was frequently sought and invariably trusted. When Richard Rowland, head of Metro, bought the film rights of the Blasco-Ibanez novel *The Four Horsemen of the Apocalypse* in 1918, he naturally turned to June Mathis for a script. It was she who suggested a leading man as well—Valentino. She later claimed that what clinched her decision was seeing him in *Eyes of Youth*. Whether they had known each other prior to this is unrecorded: but probably they had met, for at that moment Valentino, like her, was in New York working on *Stolen Moments*, a film in which he played a scoundrelly Brazilian seducer. But there is another plausible, if hypothetical reason why she should have offered the part to this relative unknown with such

*Valentino had to play yet
another villain in D. W.
Griffith's 1919 production
Out of Luck, but the
compensation was acting with
Dorothy Gish, not featured at
her best in this still*

*With Dorothy Gish in
Out of Luck. Lillian Gish
has recorded that her sister
discovered Valentino dancing
in a night-club. When she had
persuaded Griffith to cast him,
she found Valentino to be such
a fastidious dresser that he held
up shooting*

confidence. By this time Valentino was discovering his interest in—and later his gift for—spiritual communication: his mother had died the year before and the lengthy physical separation from his homeland at this lonely moment had induced him to try to get nearer her in spirit. June Mathis was a confirmed frequenter of seances, with a deep belief in reincarnation which, as we shall see, played a part in Valentino's choice of films in later years. We can only speculate whether this shared sympathy predisposed her to the young Italian, though she certainly would not have allowed her spiritual affinities to overide her professional judgment. What is certain is that there is no evidence, none at all, for any suggestion of a love affair between this rather plain woman of thirty-eight or thirty-nine and the youth in his early twenties which would account for her preferring him over others. In any case, Julio's role as first conceived was relatively minor: it was swiftly enlarged to be the male lead in the film only when all concerned saw the value of Valentino's personality and performance in adding a romantic dimension to a story that wasn't all that popular with Metro's executives. Films set in the First World War had been failing spectacularly at the box-office as America put behind it the memories of the struggle, with its separation and bereavement, and plunged into the heedless twenties. So plangently does the battlefield fatefulness resound through the last reel or so of *The Four Horsemen of the Apocalypse* that one forgets how much of the rest of it concerns the intimate emotions of love, seduction and adultery in cafés, drawing-rooms and artists' studios, settings made for Valentino.

He took the part with elation, and the $350 a week salary that went with it, and made one more film in New York. The title was prophetic, *The Wonderful Chance*, but the character again dismally unpropitious. He was a gang leader in a straw boater, with a Chaplinesque moustache and a cigarette that waggled as he spoke. Valentino exited from the film in handcuffs. When next he appeared on the screen, he was tangoing into fame and cinema history.

Few film entrances are as stunningly designed as Valentino's in *The Four Horsemen of the Apocalypse*. One minute the screen is empty: the next, *he is there*, seen in close-up, teeth clenched determinedly on a cigarillo, smoke puffed boldly down his nostrils like a stud stallion on a frosty morning. Deciding to cut in on a couple on the dance-floor, Valentino saunters over in his gaucho costume, hand on hip, tapping the man meaningfully on the shoulder, gazing with a very clear, unambiguous look at the girl, his right eyelid (which had a slight natural droop to it) quivering with ladykilling menace. Suddenly, he beats the man to the ground with his coiled stock whip and takes over the girl, guiding her into the kind of lazy tango he had often done in dancing exhibitions, both of them sagging sensually at the knees, the woman clasped to his body with unambiguous firmness. The dance ends with him pressing his mouth brutally over hers. The sequence loses nothing by being so calculatedly staged: the impact on audiences

The first appearance as a star, dancing the tango in
The Four Horsemen of the Apocalypse

was instantaneous. Apparently no one remembered having seen exactly the same sequence in a film made a few years earlier by the same director Rex Ingram. Ingram had also been June Mathis's choice to direct *The Four Horsemen of the Apocalypse* and, with her encouragement, he transferred the earlier dance scene 'bone and marrow' from the New York Bowery to a Latin American café. Ingram rehearsed Valentino in the sequence for three days and said later, 'I think the result showed it.' He was a director with an instinct for the vibratory key of a performer, who kept his camera grinding the whole scene through and then 'edited' his players' most spontaneous moments into a performance. But even if we pay him the compliment of guiding Valentino in this way, we must also acknowledge Valentino's faultless response. He shows a sudden gain in range and depth now that he has a role where his relations with women aren't based on fraudulent exploitation. It's often forgotten, in the over-emphasis given to the tango sequence in traditional gaucho costume, that *The Four Horsemen of the Apocalypse* was accepted by 1920s audiences as a sophisticated *modern* story. Julio the playboy who is made into a man by gallantry and sacrifice is a role that runs through the film from start to finish and embodies the whole of its love interest.

A frame enlargement from the film, revealing the character's evolution into a more world-weary and doomed hero of the battle-front

*Another café, another woman, another kind of lover.
Having established Valentino's no-nonsense way with women as an Argentinian gaucho, Ingram's film turns him into a sophisticated playboy in Paris—with Alice Terry*

A view of Valentino as a soldier. The Four Horsemen of the Apocalypse *rotated all facets of his personality*

A battlefield casualty: a harshly realistic shot from
The Four Horsemen of the Apocalypse

THE FOLLOWING PAGES
The Tender Lover: the affair with Alice Terry in
The Four Horsemen of the Apocalypse *is portrayed with painstaking delicacy*

All Valentino's talent and characteristics have ample opportunities for their display created for them by June Mathis, who advised him to tone down his previous 'Latinness' even further. John F. Seitz, an outstanding cinematographer, particularly with actresses, had been engaged by Ingram to give special attention to the film's female lead, Alice Terry, who was Ingram's fiancée, but his skill also flatters Valentino and lends him a beauty and attractiveness he had never been treated to in earlier, cheaper films. The glossy hair emphasises the extraordinary regularity of his features placed in perfect arrangement on the oval face. He has what Luigi Barzini calls 'the transparency of Italian faces'. Every emotion flickers visibly over the olive-smooth cast of cheek that was such an advantage to the 'Great Lover', for every woman thought she could feel such tender skin against her own. Yet when the war scenes require him to wear a week's growth of beard, there appears a haggard, introspective look that he could have used with profit in parts that called for a low-life look.

But it is the economy of Valentino's amorous gestures, almost imperceptible in their easy fluency, which carries the charge of sexual captivation. His love-making techniques have now the opportunity to display themselves to the full as the scene shifts to Paris, where Julio is in turn a bohemian painter, man-about-town, dandified non-combatant, repentant volunteer and battlefield fatality who finally returns from the dead in his fiancée's vision.

The first surprise is how well he modulates his romantic approach in each mood and scene so as to reflect the character of the girl to whom he is making love. He is a very varied kind of romancer, contrary to the one-fell-swoop lover of popular tradition. He raises a married woman's hand to his lips with just the right degree of deliberation that warns her of something illicit and irresistible. Valentino was naturally short-sighted, like many film stars of the silent screen whose poor sight was not helped by the glaring Klieg lights then in use before the mercury vapour lights came in. But a visual handicap actually became an advantage on the screen: it suggested intense concentration on the object Valentino *could* see, generally a woman. His mime constantly confers compliments on her as when in a chic restaurant scene—'The

BELOW
Jean Acker, the star's first wife. Marriage did not survive the first night

world was dancing,' pants the silent film caption, 'Paris had succumbed to the mad rhythm of the Argentine tango'—he delicately takes a vase with a rosebud that his beloved has just inhaled and puts it to his own nostrils to sniff the perfume, as if her own fragrance had been transferred to its petals. His direct look at the camera takes us into his confidence before he nods his assent to her plea that he will promise to be good if she goes back to his apartment. There is no brutality in Valentino's approaches, though he never lets us forget who is master from the way he presses the woman's head back as he kisses her and sucks his cheeks in ever so slightly. He is a mixture of passion and playfulness, giving an impish pat to Alice Terry's stockinged feet as he helps her off with her wet shoes, or raising two fingers with an almost Chaplinesque gesture of feminineness as he pours out her tea, kissing the sugar lump before dropping it in—a Monsieur Verdoux in his young days, before the onset of cynicism.

Before the film even opened publicly, other producers were sending out 'feelers' to Valentino. As show business still says, 'the news was out'—a star was in the making. The star himself, however, outside the excitement of immersing himself totally in a role in a worthy film, had very little to make him feel a happy, complete man. For at the very moment his charms were being exercised in the conquest of women on the screen, and soon everywhere in America and in most places abroad which boasted a box-office, his new wife was shutting the door of her room in the Hollywood Hotel in his face, putting up the chain, and informing him that their impulsive marriage of a few hours earlier had been a terrible mistake.

The woman whom Valentino had met in November 1919, and impulsively proposed to and married a few days later, was a young Metro actress called Jean Acker. That she shut her door in his face on their wedding night is known from sworn evidence given at their divorce two years later. What remains to be guessed at is why both parties were so obviously ill-mated from the start. There are clues in Jean Acker's impressionable character and the ambiguous status she held at the time. She had called herself a purely 'decorative' film actress; in fact she was extremely closely attached to Metro's leading

female star of the time, the exotic, Russian-born Alla Nazimova. A somewhat snidely phrased paragraph in the September 1919, issue of *Photoplay* reported: 'Nazimova in her recent trip to New York brought back to Los Angeles a series of celluloid frogs and toads which she toys with as she takes her regular Saturday nights. In addition she discovered a new brand of perfumed cigarettes, together with a protégé (*sic*) who used to be known to the world as Jeanne Acker, but who now prefers to call herself Jeanne Mendoza.' Now for any actress to change her name from plain 'Acker' to glamorous 'Mendoza' is simply part of Hollywood's folkways. But in this case it also complied with the more intimate self-posturings and affectations of the circle of women round Nazimova, a lesbian of managerial will and temper whose word was law on the Metro lot until even they could stomach no more. Her production of *Salome*, in 1923, was cast as far as possible entirely from homosexual players, in homage to Wilde, and it effectively bankrupted her, thus ending her independent artistic imperium. It was designed, incidentally, by another of her protégées, Natacha Rambova, who had been born Winnifred Shaughnessy, in Salt Lake City, and who was destined to be Valentino's second wife. Thus a great deal of the power and influence later brought to bear on Valentino derives directly from the Nazimova connection, including, one guesses, the rule that sex should be subservient to art and be used in a way that sustained the affections without contracting the more normal responsibilities that go with a heterosexual relationship.

In this dedicated but highly competitive court circle where Nazimova, at the height of her power as a star and being paid $13,000 a week, would rotate her favourites, a minor talent like Jean Acker was bound to feel confused, insecure and frequently rejected. It was in such a mood that she apparently said yes to Valentino's proposal: it was a marriage of convenience, of companionship on her part, which immediately broke down once the consequence of having to share the marriage bed could no longer be postponed. Later on she charged him with physically assaulting her and with being unable to support her financially. Valentino certainly had a strong and petulant temper: he was extremely thin skinned and any insult to his vanity resulted in a flare-up, which was just as quickly doused by some distracting word of flattery or appeasement. But Jean Acker's evidence proved so dubious under cross-examination that it has to be viewed very sceptically. What is beyond doubt is that the marriage was over and done with inside a few hours, leaving Valentino to draw the sting out of his wounded and remorseful feelings by hard work. More interesting, though, is the position he now found himself in with three women: June Mathis, Nazimova and Natacha Rambova. Each of them was tied to the others by strong bonds of temperamental affinity and professional interest. Mathis had scripted three Nazimova films, Rambova was her brilliant production designer. And all three of them had advance knowledge of Valentino's capacities as an actor, a romantic leading man, and his potential as a star. He was drawn even closer into the circle by the offer of the chief male role opposite Nazimova in *Camille*, which Natacha Rambova was designing as a modern-dress, art-deco drama.

'I was hunting for a young man to play Armand,' Nazimova recalled many years later, when she was assisting her own 'comeback' by remembering the now legendary figure who had co-starred with her in the 1920s. 'I had already interviewed scores of young men, but none seemed to match my idea of a romantic star. Even Valentino didn't. He was fat and far too swarthy. His bushy black eyebrows were grotesque. Yet I saw that if he could reduce and pluck his eyebrows, he would be the perfect Latin lover. He did just that.' Apart from the likelihood that it was June Mathis and Natacha Rambova who did the actual

Valentino followed The Four Horsemen of the Apocalypse *with an Arctic melodrama* Uncharted Seas *co-starring Alice Lake*

'hunting' for her, this suggests Nazimova's domineering tone well enough. Valentino was 'vetted' by her and Rambova as he stood in front of them in Arctic furs, for he had come straight from the set of *Uncharted Seas*, a routine 'outdoor' melodrama he had plunged into immediately after completing *The Four Horsemen of the Apocalypse*, probably simply to earn more ready money for what he suspected—rightly—would be Jean Acker's financial claims on his meagre assets. As well as recommending a diet and depilatory treatment, the two women at once shampooed Valentino's shiny black skullcap of hair and fluffed it out with hot tongs till it was more the style that a young French provincial like Armand, who was well-born but no 'ladykiller', might have affected. After a screen test, they gave him the part.

With Alice Lake in Uncharted Seas: *he was still in a state of 'deep freeze' when Nazimova interviewed him to play opposite her in* Camille

For obvious reasons Jean Acker wouldn't have been on the set while *Camille* was being shot, but by this time she was very much the ex-protégée. Natacha Rambova was in the ascendant, and not simply in Nazimova's affections. Though the director of *Camille* was nominally Ray Smallwood, it was in fact Rambova's advice, as well as her designs, which the Russian star followed implicitly. Thus Valentino, too, came under the influence of this gifted, narcissistic, exceptionally strong-willed woman whose production designs reveal her as one of the era's pioneers in film and costume décor. She used a curvilinear motif in *Camille*, sensually and luxuriously 'modern' in, say, the Paris apartment set with its semi-circular glass bedroom doors, lights depending from the ceiling like stalactites, and low, round, wide-arched doorways leading into orgiastic dinner-parties which took place against the perpetual snowscape of the city outside. Into such designs the players have to fit themselves: the stylistic dominance that Natacha Rambova was later to try and wield over her future husband's career is already evident in the first film that linked their names. Throughout it Valentino is subordinated to Nazimova on whom the accent of exoticism and perverseness is firmly set. From the very first he is a pliant suppliant, not a seducer, forever dropping on to one knee to signify his fidelity, and quite bowled over by his first vision of her ('I wish I were a dog so that I might care for you.') As well he might. For Nazimova in her lizard-tail opera dress *is* extraordinary, her very small, lean, sinewy, ballet-dancer's body zig-zagging through Natacha Rambova's curving décor while her huge curly head, tossed wilfully back or inclining over a female protégée with a hint of Lesbian affection that the more sophisticated audiences would get, perpetually threatens to break off at the neck. She had imported a Russian photographer specialising in soft-focus for the film, for she was already in her forties, and the camerawork continually favours her. Valentino has to take his tempo from her, too. Yet the earliest hint of what was to become one of his most seductive features occurs in this film. It is when he breaks the bank in a gambling casino—he's been playing to kill the pain of losing Camille—and with a sudden, unanticipated flash of cruelty he seizes her arms, forces them behind her and pinions them there while he plants a kiss on her lips. This was the 'cruel' Valentino. This was the so called 'sex-menace'. This was the element of 'threat' in him that worked its way to the top of the scale of romantic emotions he stirred up in the hearts of women. He could be, he *must* be kind to a woman—but they liked him to be cruel, just a *little* cruel to her first. By the time the filming was over Valentino had fallen completely in love with Natacha Rambova, impressed by her passion for detail and her European culture. His own innately romantic disposition which thought in terms of stardom and his public fell under the spell of a woman with the mind of a man which thought in terms of Art and serving her Muse. The 'Great Lover' was himself seduced. . . .

STAFFORDSHIRE LIBRARY

With Nazimova in an up-dated Camille. *Natacha Rambova's art-deco setting embraces them both*

The lovers in Camille. *The 'iris' effect and the extremely soft-focus photography are characteristic of the film*

4

THERE IS LITTLE record of the early girl-hood of Winnifred Shaughnessy, but the second marriage of her mother's, to Richard Hudnut, the cosmetics tycoon, gave the girl a fatal entrée to European culture. She was sent to school in England, at Leatherhead Court, near Epsom, where she excelled in drawing, painting and music, and the wilfulness that later marked her film career showed itself dramatically when she ran away from school and eluded all efforts to find her, including those of private detectives and American consuls. According to some reports, she arrived in pre-Revolutionary Russia, where she met Theodore Kosloff who was then with the Imperial ballet. When Kosloff visited the United States with his own ballet troupe, she went with him, using the *nom de danse* of Natacha Rambova. She was there when the Russian Revolution broke out and she stayed on, though no longer employed by Kosloff with whom she had had a characteristic falling-out. She found her way to Hollywood where her skill in teaching the Russian star Nazimova how to dance, as well as her own originality as a designer, gave her a secure niche in the film industry. She put her career before all else: even before marriage, which she considered a risk to her talents. The imper-manent art of acting she held in lower esteem than the chance it gave her to design the production around it; a view that was particularly ominous for the career of her future husband and their life together. And as well as her love of culture, which was quite genuine and extensive, Natacha had picked up something else in Europe—she was a snob. To the end of her days she vented her dislike of the uncouth Hollywood folk—Nazimova and her *intimes* apart—and characterised the film colony as 'one continuous struggle of nobodies to become somebodies, all pretending to be what they are not'. (Such 'pretence' is pitching it rather strong, coming from someone who preserved her own 'Russian' persona until her marriage to Valentino forced her to reveal who she was.) She also scorned her future husband's infatuation with the movies, or, at least, the popular American movies. Part of the later strain that developed between them came from Natacha's attempt to steer his career towards the European 'art film' in which the players were a part of the total artistic concept and not 'merely' stars who embodied the movie's whole commercial appeal in their personalities. She often poked fun at the way Valentino tried to tell American jokes: it's hardly surprising to learn that she had no sense of humour herself, none at all. Garbo had more recorded wit.

What, then, *did* they have in common? Well, dancing for one thing. Though Natacha considered the school in which she had learnt to dance was a purer as well as a more imperial one than the *thé-dansants* which had sponsored her husband's footwork, both of them were excellent partners on the dance floor, a talent of immense usefulness to them in later days when the film studio suspended Valentino and he had to find some means to keep himself before the public. Touring with his wife and giving displays of exhibition dancing proved the answer: and if Natacha felt this a bit *infra dig*, she also felt the need of money. Then both of them loved animals and kept a veritable menagerie at one time, including a stable of horses, a police dog puppy, a Peke, a Dobermann Pinscher, two Great Danes (his engagement gift to her), lion cubs, a monkey and a pet snake. And they shared a deep interest in spiritualism, which may have been their strongest tie. Natacha was a passionate devotee of astrology and the stars' influence on her life and work. Along with June Mathis and Nazimova she took part in Hollywood seances which reinforced the sense of power that these women turned into very real influence in their dealings with the studios. Valentino discovered early on in his career that he was able to receive spirit messages and practise automatic writing with some success; and a 'familiar' called 'Black Feather', who represented himself as a Redskin brave, became his 'guide' and was consulted by the star before making any important move.

He was still a newcomer in 1921. He had made a hit in *The Four Horsemen of the Apocalypse*, but it might be a 'onc-off' hit. Who was to say his success was going to grow? He was a new type: had he got what it took to be a star? *Camille* was not the sort of film to reinforce his debut—it was not *his* film, to begin with—and he found that his part in the next film, a June Mathis adaptation of Balzac's *Eugenie Grandet* renamed *The Conquering Power*, had suffered severe pruning at the hands of its director, Rex Ingram. This may seem surprising. After all, hadn't Ingram lavished attention on him in *The Four Horsemen of the Apocalypse*? He had; and had paid for it by seeing his 'star' steal the notices, not only from him, who had made him what he was (as Ingram thought), but from Ingram's fiancée, Alice Terry, who was also with the cast of *The Conquering Power*. Ingram, it would seem, didn't wish for the same experience again. Looking back in 1949 on those days, he recalled that Valentino was 'just a good looking, lucky guy who copped a sensational role (as Julio) and a good cameraman . . . It was a surefire role of a Spanish gigolo (*sic*) . . . it would have made anyone who was cast properly'. It's doubtful if *The Conquering Power* would have 'made' anyone, properly cast or not. The attention is settled firmly on to the woman's role and Valentino has little to do except cut a fashion-plate figure (which he does easily), complete with a monocle and a dog on a lead. The story removes him from the film for a long stretch by sending him to Martinique, returning him to mainland France only in the closing stages and then as an ageing man with a cane and a beard, though the actor's slower, more 'elderly' movements are evidence, even in long shot, of Valentino's power to suggest character by very economical means. But the film did nothing for him. And his vanity was also hit when Metro refused him a $100 a week rise.

It must have been round about this time, as Kevin Brownlow reports in *The Parade's Gone By*, that the great French filmmaker Abel Gance, visiting Hollywood, met a depressed and embittered Valentino who begged to be taken back to France with him and put in films there. ' "I'm fed up with this place,' he said. 'There's a terrible feel about it all. It's so artificial. I want to get back to Europe." ' Gance advised Valentino to stay put: he was doing very well in Hollywood. He was, but it's when one is 'doing very well' that one is impatient to do even better. Following Metro's refusal to pay him more, Valentino took drastic action. He went to see Jesse Lasky at the Famous Players–Lasky company, later Paramount, and blurted out angrily how Metro was wronging him. Lasky was impressed—Valentino in an Italian tantrum was said to be like a miniature Vesuvius—and at once ordered his contracts department to draw up a five-year agreement, starting at $500 a week, which the star signed before he left. Such, anyhow, is the usual story that gets into the biographies. It is almost certainly incorrect. First of all, a man like Lasky, well used to the fancied injustices of film performers, and even more alert to the possible legal risks of signing up someone else's employee, would not have taken Valentino's word there and then as authorisation to do the deed, acquire a star and spite a rival outfit. It is much more likely that news of Valentino's discontent had been carried to Lasky much earlier by none other than June Mathis, who also now joined him at a studio where she could expect to have more power and bigger budgets than at Metro which had only been saved from threatening bankruptcy by the unforeseen success of *The Four Horsemen of the Apocalypse*. June Mathis knew just how such deals worked: they were sweetened if a talent like Valentino was part of them. This has a much clearer ring of truth than the tale of a discontented star making a deal by berating his old employer for underpaying him: an approach that would be more likely to put any new employer on his guard directly. The one person put out by the move was Natacha Rambova, who reproached Valentino for accepting less than a thousand dollars a week starting salary. Soon she had another cause for displeasure. The first subject in which it was proposed to star Valentino was a lurid piece of bookstall fiction that Natacha deemed 'utter trash'. Its title: *The Sheik*.

The Sheik was the film that assured Valentino's life-time patent on the 'Great Lover'. It was the film that projected his fantasy image as a romantic menace whose finer feelings towards the woman he enslaved

PREVIOUS PAGE
Beginning of the myth: shooting starts on The Sheik

Revolver versus cigarette holder: most stills from The Sheik *catch its unfortunately 'camp' characteristics* . . .

redeemed the male chauvinism that led him to possess her in the first place. By putting only one woman, Lady Diana Mayo, within the power of an Arab who could traditionally have been expected to maintain a harem of them, Edith M. Hull's novel allowed every female reader to project herself into the heroine's role and so increase the wishful identification. The confrontation between male and female was heightened by the isolated setting in the desert and by the directness of approach by a seeming 'barbarian' who assumed that the victim he had abducted from her horse to his ('Lie still, you little fool') knew what it was all about. 'Why have you brought me here?' she demands, once they're in his tent. 'Are you not woman enough to know?' he answers sarcastically. Over a million English-speaking readers, and as many more in other languages, certainly were. Basically pornographic in its teasing dwelling on the physical humiliation that was half desired by the helpless woman, *The Shiek*'s emotional impact was enhanced by the timing of its publication. The theme appealed directly to the liberated 'New Woman' of the 1920s who wore her skirts shorter and her hair bobbed, who smoked, danced, drank from her beau's hip flask and took up every fad or craze of a novelty era. To buy and read *The Sheik* was a way of flaunting one's emancipation. At the same time the book appealed to other women—perhaps many more of these—who clung to the traditions of family and marriage and social convention and wanted simply to experience the thrill without the commitment to its consequences. For *The Sheik* not only exploited sexual sadism: it also legitimised the desert liaison by revealing Ahmed Ben Hassan to be, below the burnous and the desert tan, none other than a Scottish nobleman, the Earl of Glencarryl, who had been abandoned in the Sahara as a baby. Over the barbaric fantasy, the book laid an aristocratic one. Blue blood restored the commercial viability of a film subject that might have been impaired at the box-office by an insistence on mixed blood. All these elements the film adaptation preserved—though her repugnance for the subject caused June Mathis to beg off early on—and they flew like magnetic particles on to Valentino. It was helpful, too, to have *The Sheik* released in October–November 1921, thus catching the full force of the public sensation he had made only a few months earlier in *The Four Horsemen of the Apocalypse* which had been held back from the screen to coincide with the dedication of the grave of the Unknown Warrior at Mount Arlington national cemetery.

Compared with the sensitivity Valentino had shown in that film, *The Sheik* is a crude comic-strip. He knew this and always detested it. He confessed he was confused about how to play the role—as a Latin, as an Arab, or as a latent English Milord? This time there was no Rex Ingram to offer guidance, only George Melford, an action director who went for the main chance in every scene.

Yet such crudity is part and parcel of the film's power and much of Valentino's, too. His virility is emphasised at all points, even

. . . but audiences, particularly women, savoured the audacity of the desert lover who could humble proud Agnes Ayres . . .

. . . and when the Son of the Sheik's arms were finally around his true love, Vilma Banky, women practically felt Valentino's lips against their own cheeks

enhanced with the phallic symbolism of the Sheik's cigarette holder (not a customary Arab accoutrement at this date) which ends up on 'the morning after' among the disarray of combs and brushes on the lady's dressing-table in her desert tent. The film, though, makes it clear that no rape has taken place: that would have mortally damaged the erotic fantasy. Valentino's acting is as functionally emphatic as the huge curved dagger in his waist-band: it emphasises his aggressive masculinity. His grin is the size of a slice of Spanish melon; his eyelids look suspiciously as if they've been gummed back to expose more of the passionate 'whites', though this occasionally produces an unfortunate 'pop-eyed' effect. Yet the Sheik's aim isn't simply to humiliate his captive. Lady Diana, played by Agnes Ayres, comes into the film a militant feminist, 'beautiful, unconventional, spurning love as a weakness,' as the titles tell us, yet after an hour or two with her abductor she is exchanging her riding breeches for a skirt ('You make a charming boy,' he tells her, 'but it was not a boy I saw in Biskra') and she gradually recovers her femininity until she can say in a celebrated line that became a catch-phrase of the time, a sure sign of its mythical status, 'I am not afraid with your arms around me, Ahmed, my desert love, MY SHEIK.' (It was a line that the males in the audience had no response to: it asked the women to identify with Agnes Ayres and simply left the men feeling outclassed by Valentino. In it lies the making of much of the male antipathy he later suffered.)

'Shriek—For The Sheik Will Seek You Too!' cried the publicity posters less because it was deemed necessary to make such an erotic promise than because many film-goers might still be uncertain how to pronounce the name. The woman who could fancy herself as a rape-object and end up as a love-object and feeling more womanly for it: to such a one the film delivered the full force of what one reviewer called Valentino's 'Latin subtlety and verve (blazing) to sudden rage with impressive conviction and as readily (flashing) white teeth with nomadic frankness.'

The star-making machine now began to run at full power. Box-office returns soon alerted Lasky to just what sort of phenomenon he had got. Fan magazines were booming by this date and the studio fed them every available tidbit of news about *The Sheik*. Newspapers, too, had realised by now the grip that Hollywood had on their readers and *The Sheik* (and Valentino) had that wonderful adaptability beloved by newspaper department editors and make-up men which fitted into any column that was going, from the women's pages to the week-end competitions. Even the sheet-music industry cashed in on the phenomenon with *The Sheik of Araby*; and the surest sign that a new trend in popular taste had been located was the appearance of other desert dramas and dusky Pretenders like *Arabian Love* with John Gilbert, *Arab* with Ramon Novarro and *Song of Love* with Edmund Carewe.

Valentino's divorce from Jean Acker coincided with *The Sheik*'s release and did him no harm at all. On the contrary, when his estranged wife testified that 'he hit me with his fist and knocked me down' millions of women simply sighed and wished that they, too, had been dealt such love-blows. *The Sheik*'s sensational success in fact distracted the public from the curiosity some of them might have felt about a 'Great Lover' whose wife had locked him out of the bedroom on their wedding night. What was more disturbing to Valentino's new employers was the sworn evidence he had had to give about Natacha Rambova's influence on his work, on his choice of parts and the way he played them. He had been obliged to mention this so as to rebut the innuendoes arising out of a photograph circulated in court which showed him dressed as a faun, with nothing on except a skin-fitting pair of simulated fur tights, playing a flute and capering in a rather camp fashion. It was alleged that this was how he had disported himself with Natacha Rambova instead of supporting his wife. Valentino tried to explain it away as a 'costume test' for a film called *The Faun Through the Ages* which had ultimately come to nothing. If any such film project existed, no light has since been shed on it. What is much more likely, knowing Natacha's ballet background, is that the photographs were attempting to duplicate the posture and appearance of Nijinsky's angular choreography for his own ballet *L'Après-midi d'un Faune*. Quite possibly Natacha saw Nijinsky dance—he was at the Metropolitan Opera in 1916—and may have been 'trying out' Valentino in a ballet which she admired, though it was one which the public had rejected. It shows how her mind was running at this time. The photograph closely resembles ones taken of Nijinsky by Bert and Baron de Meyer. Any more lubricous explanation for Valentino's masquerade doesn't survive scrutiny: it's not a very orgiastic looking faun, and no matching nymph has ever been discovered.

Meanwhile Lasky had rushed his new star into a modern-dress romantic drama, *Moran of the Lady Letty*, in which he played a San Francisco socialite. This time it is the man who is abducted in his spotless week-end sailor's rig aboard the Lady Letty and learns to take life less frivolously through hard work and love for Moran the skipper's daughter. Natacha again disliked the script—'Modern stories always bored me to tears,' she confided in her memoirs—and Valentino was never keen on the finished film. He felt it diminished his romantic allure to put him into contemporary dress. Yet his performance is an exceptionally fine one, very well shaded dramatically, and because most of the film was shot in ordinary lighting and without make-up on the San Francisco waterfront, where square-riggers still produced the effect of a floating forest and a bijou kinema on the pier is showing Louis Feuillade's serial *Fantomas*, it's among Valentino's most natural and likeable characterisations. It's also one designed to show off his manliness *among men*, which lends likelihood to the story that Lasky was already anxious about the male backlash against his star from those who had been dragged to see *The Sheik* by wives or

Valentino as Nijinsky, a performance not intended for the public

The real Nijinsky in L'Après-midi d'un Faune

As a tough sailor in Moran of the Lady Letty. *Valentino felt that such 'modern dress' movies diminished his romantic appeal: certainly the pipe did not add anything to it*

Moran of the Lady Letty *was intended to establish Valentino's appeal as more than a 'lady's man' with American males. Here his virility is put to the test by Walter Long*

Valentino as a Redskin. He delighted in dressing up for new parts, which never got on the screen, and feeling himself inside an alien skin. This one, he felt, brought him a closer spiritual kinship with the Indian brave, Black Feather, who was his psychic 'guide'

girlfriends and were resenting the amorous conquests of 'the dago'. Valentino proves more than equal to the rough-and-tumble challenge, his muscles rippling under his sailor's singlet, hoisting up his bellbottoms like a tough street-navvy spoiling for a fight, and throwing punches or receiving them in a mighty running battle with a villainous captain along the deck, up the mast and even out on the yardarm like Doug Fairbanks Sr. His expression in moments of menace, eyes narrowed to distrustful slits and cheeks like granite, recalls the 'great stone face' of another of his star contemporaries W. S. Hart. Though his love scenes with Dorothy Dalton require him to put his drawing-room etiquette behind him, his gentleness is always on call—he plucks her sleeve like a puppy attracting its mistress's attention, then kisses her ever so tenderly while his ex-fiancée from the San Francisco smart set glides by unwittingly on her private yacht. Even such a minor trait as the rolling gait he's acquired aboard ship following him on to dry land at the end, as an earnest of his conversion to honest, homely, hard-working ways, shows the care Valentino took in thinking his roles through and sustaining them.

The film, however, didn't do too well at the box-office, which confirmed Valentino's feeling that his future roles should be costume ones. Costumes for him and, even more, for Natacha were part of the spectacle that sent his imagination racing. They transformed him in more than outward appearance. They gave him a near-psychic feeling that he was in touch with the era they represented. Historical flashbacks were deliberately introduced into his contemporary films wherever possible: even his modern dress *Camille* had managed to present its twentieth-century Marguerite and Armand as Manon and Des Grieux in a sequence in which they imagined themselves to be the characters in *Manon Lescaut*. Later films set in contemporary times like *The Young Rajah* and *Cobra* had their 'period pieces' too. All this was connected with the belief that he, Natacha Rambova and June Mathis, as well as others in their circle, shared in the transmigration and reincarnation of souls. A previous existence, invariably in a more 'dressy' age, was therefore invented for the characters in some of the Valentino vehicles who were otherwise confined to modern souls in

Valentino in Chinese make-up. He never played such a role, but enjoyed experimenting. He also greatly admired Richard Barthelmess's performance as the Chinaman in Griffith's 1919 production Broken Blossoms, *and Valentino's Oriental look strongly resembles the latter's, not least in the ultra-soft focus used in both film and photo*

contemporary bodies. Valentino's 'mental make-up' was so psychic, according to Natacha's memoirs, that just donning a costume gave him the feeling of entering into communication with someone in an earlier existence. On an actor's already highly suggestible imagination, this woman certainly worked hard and was continuously, helped, as she frequently observed, by the fact that Valentino was 'a child'. The word 'child' recurs so often in her memoirs that it must have been her habitual way of thinking of him. It's one, we may note, that precludes any sexual intimations. 'With his childish enthusiasm and sincerity,' she wrote, 'he could make you see wonders in anything in which he was interested at the moment.' This suggests the 'love of show' which Luigi Barzini considered an essential part of the Italian character. 'How many impossible things become probable here,' Barzini has written in his study of his countrymen, 'how many insuperable difficulties can be smoothed over with the right clothes, the right facial expression, the right *mis-en-scène*, the right words?' He might have been describing the whole make-believe of film stardom. Natacha's memoirs are stuffed with tributes to the 'love of show', with descriptions of the clothes, furnishings and *objets d'art* that she and Valentino would buy up in vast quantities on tours in Europe for later use in his films or in their own dwelling houses. At times one feels that both of them had that gluttony for rich surfaces that Wilde revealed in writing *Salome*.

Towards the end of 1921 another woman used her considerable influence to Valentino's advantage—by endorsing his sex appeal. Madame Elinor Glyn, the Edwardian novelist, authoress of *Three Weeks* and other (in their time) daring works, had been co-opted by Hollywood as a shield of respectability against the critics of film industry's morals. While in the film colony she not only earned herself large fees of up to £500 a week for public lectures on romantic love, but also 'supervised' some film versions of her own and other writers' books, leaning imperiously on an authentic reproduction of the niceties of social etiquette, and she claimed to be able to divine which stars had what it took to be good screen lovers. This quality was later known as 'It' when Madame Glyn discovered it in Clara Bow; and now she approved of 'It'—the 'Ur—It', surely—in Valentino who, not quite fortuitously perhaps, was playing in Madame's version of *Beyond the Rocks*. She taught him an additional trick for the film, kissing a lady's palm instead of the back of her hand, and she underwrote his reputation for menace with her ideal of romantic love. Valentino gratefully let her 'ghost' parts of an article in *Photoplay* for March 1922, which resonates with 'Glyn-isms' like 'The most difficult thing in the world is to make a man love you when he sees you every day', and 'Nothing interferes with romance like restlessness.' She also skilfully worked in a few of Valentino's more masculinely slanted shibboleths: 'One can always be kind to a woman one cares nothing about—and to a woman by whom one is attracted. But only cruel to a woman one loves or has loved.' Such shrewd publicising of his commitment to the romantic ethic helped boost Valentino's fan mail to over a thousand letters a week.

Valentino was very conscious of the scar on his right cheek: it did not always show up as clearly as it does in this portrait study— perhaps he felt that it went with the pirate-like head-dress

His favourite role, as Juan Gallardo, the bullfighter in Blood and Sand. *The man behind the camera is director Fred Niblo*

After his shipboard toughening course in Moran of the Lady Letty, *it was back to playing an English milord in the Elinor Glyn story* Beyond the Rocks

In January 1922, his divorce case was decided in his favour. Jean Acker had 'deserted' him. But he had to muster over $12,000 to settle her 'quit' claim, a sum which Lasky advanced him, believing that it was no bad thing for stars to be in their studio's debt in more ways than one. Money was both weapon and reward in Hollywood; and the ever-increasing debts run up by 'difficult' players were welcomed and sometimes connived at by the front office as a way of establishing 'good will' when the studio met the bills or, if this didn't work, of bringing the ingrates smartly to heel. Valentino was now earning $1,250 weekly, but spending much and owing thousands in legal fees. The Rambova memoirs, if they are to be believed, speak of the pair of them living mainly on love and spaghetti (which they cooked in her little Sunset Boulevard bungalow) and even getting up at dawn to hunt for their dinner by shooting doves or quail on nearby ranch land. Natacha had still not publicly revealed that she was a cosmetic tycoon's stepdaughter: even when she did in May 1922, when she and Valentino announced their engagement, it doesn't appear that her parents came through with anything more solid than joy at the return of a daughter and pride at the acquisition of such a celebrity as their son-in-law. They were married on 13 May. Eight days later the new husband was arrested in Los Angeles on a bigamy charge and thrown in jail.

Valentino had failed to heed the requirement of a full year that Californian law decreed must elapse between divorce and re-marriage. The charge was dismissed early in June for lack of evidence of co-habitation, which in itself set tongues wagging. But though the legal tangle was serio-comic, his imprisonment even for a matter of hours permanently scarred Valentino's self-esteem: it was too close for his liking to his earlier, mercifully less publicised incarceration in the Tombs prison in New York. Why Lasky had let him go to jail at all, till friends stood bail for him, baffled and angered him and was the cause of his first serious breach with his employer. Perhaps the film chief felt that a few hours' reflection in a jail cell would cool down his hot-tempered star; while a marital mix-up with a millionaire's stepdaughter would hardly hurt his image with fans who believed that romantic love overcame all, even the interlocutory powers of California's divorce laws. It was no bad thing, either, to have Valentino's name in headlines so near the première date of his new film, *Blood and Sand*.

5

FOR VALENTINO TO be a virile figure wasn't enough. *Moran of the Lady Letty* had proved that. He must be menacing, too. *Blood and Sand* looks as if it was intended to be a masterly corrective, a definitive shaping of his appeal as the *homme fatal* inflicting pain as well as suffering it. Adapted once again by June Mathis from the Ibañez story of the peasant bullfighter who is seduced and betrayed by a vamp and then vanquished by the bull, a sense of darkening destiny is built into it. It is not a love story so much as a career story in which the women who threaten to come between Valentino and his destiny in the bullring first elicit his ruthless rejection of them—and then (and then only) his repentant lover's reflex. The accent is put on suffering, not seduction. Valentino takes the floor in a big dance sequence, obviously paralleling that in *The Four Horsemen of the Apocalypse*, heels clicking, body bent like an archers bow, hands on hips; but as his vampish partner tilts her lips up to him expectantly, his mouth curls and he flings her away. Up comes the dialogue title: 'I hate all women. . . .' In place of *The Sheik*'s bold abduction, there is a seduction scene of great archness in which a miscast Nita Naldi—the lady of the novel was a blonde whose passion for the dark-skinned matador was an attraction of opposites—vamps a morose Valentino in an atmosphere of incense, draped tapestries and a black slave to light his cigars. 'Snake!' he cries. 'One minute I love you—the next I hate you.' The strong-weak man ends up with his head in her lap: real passion he reserves for the arena. Valentino however makes an excellent Spaniard: again it's a creation quite distinct from all previous ones. His very hands appear to have been enlarged for the peasant's part, they suggest the youth's awkwardness so dexterously—except, that is, when he has a sword in them. His eyebrows have been thickened till they appear to meet, giving his brow an unaccustomed heaviness. He darkens the man's character imaginatively, first appearing with a mischievous air as a bullring urchin with full curly hair, tattered pants and boyish aplomb. With the onset of ambition, he grows into resplendent virility, hair glistening like a black pond in moonlight, sideburns sharpened into wicked stiletto points.

The Brutal Lover: **Blood and Sand** *rings the changes on the 'love and hate' personality of the matador who inflicts pain on the woman who sets out to vamp him—and suffers some himself from her own sharp-toothed retort. Valentino and Nita Naldi*

The final pact in Blood and Sand *was made with Death, not with a woman. It pleased audiences all the more to feel that a tragic end put him beyond reach of a possibly unworthy female*

As the slyly humorous bullring urchin before turning into the elegant dragon-fly of a matador. The light-bodied grace is visible beneath the rags

The lady-killing look in Blood and Sand: *the eyebrows have been thickened till they virtually meet, but the bandana handkerchief preserves the 'skull-cap' sleekness of the more familiar patent-leather hair. So mesmerising was the power of Valentino's eyes that audiences quite overlooked his protuberant ears*

Some of Valentino's films from now on feature him dressing or undressing, displaying his physique and teasing his fans with the hinted exposure. Later on he made a fly little self-parody out of this in a short that shows him arriving on the sea-shore in a limousine, stripping in the car and then pulling down the car blind at the last minute with an impish *moue*. *Blood and Sand* shows him being dressed for the *corrida* in his 'suit of lights', his extremities protruding sexily from behind a screen until he emerges into view swivelling on his heels to let his cummerbund be wrapped round his neat waist. It resembles the demonstrations of pugilistic prowess he later felt compelled to give in any handy boxing-ring in order to rebut the charges of effeminacy levelled at him by gossip-writers capitalising on male jealousy. This trend of his set in early with the tenacity of a neurosis. He had good cause for thought. Even while *Blood and Sand* was being shot, the April 1922, issue of *Photoplay* carried a boorish lampoon of *The Sheik* 'whose mother was a wop or something like that.' And the same writer really let fly in the July issue—had the arrogant Spanish manners Valentino assumed for the screen carried over into his Press interviews?—when he published a litany of 'hate' against the star 'I hate Valentino! All men hate Valentino. I hate his oriental optics; I hate his classic nose; I hate his Roman face; I hate his smile; I hate his glistening teeth; I hate his patent-leather hair; I hate his Svengali glare; I hate him because he dances too well; I hate him because he's a slicker; I hate him because he's the great lover of the screen; I hate him because he's an embezzler of hearts; I hate him because he's too apt in the art of osculation; I hate him because he's leading man for

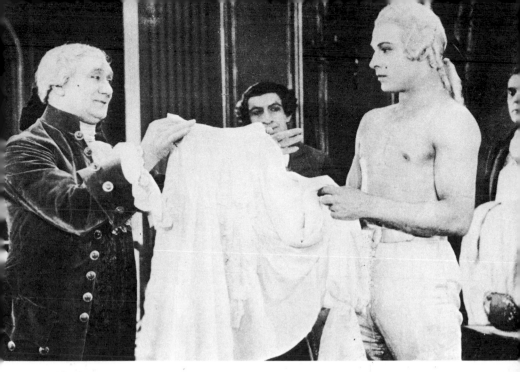

The cult of the body. Valentino valued his physical prowess and took every opportunity to display it. Dressing scenes were relished, particularly when they could be associated with the display of costumes, as in Blood and Sand *and* Monsieur Beaucaire

Gloria Swanson; I hate him because he's too good-looking.'

The truth was that Valentino had made lovemaking into too onerous and time-consuming a task for American males to emulate. He had shown the Latin trait of infinite consideration in his courtship which requires an equivalent amount of time, patience and vanity. It wasn't the American ideal, at least it wasn't the American *male* ideal. To American women, though, it was part of the process of 'liberation' to surrender yourself to an un-American male: by his very difference in approach, he reinforced their desire, which Madame Glyn had actively promoted to her profit and Cecil B. DeMille's early 'society' films had insisted on, that husbands should be constant lovers and that romance shouldn't end with marriage. The average American male couldn't imagine himself as a French nobleman, an Argentine gaucho, an Arab sheik or a Russian cossack, or any of Valentino's other exotic roles; but the women in the audience found it much easier to identify with the women in Valentino's embrace. To the feminine psyche, his alien exoticism was intriguing: to the male drive, it was competitive and inhibiting. Compared with this Latin, the American was the 'lousy lover'.

By mid-1922, Valentino's relations with Lasky were cooling. The star was asserting that the studio was out to exploit his notoriety and ruin

SHOALHAVEN SHIRE LIBRARY

Carrying the college boat in an early scene from The Young
Rajah *enabled Valentino to display more of his body appeal, even
if the costume that went with it was scarcely the 'historical' kind
he usually assumed. It is this photo that reputedly led to the
vetting of stills displayed outside local cinemas*

Jack Dempsey acts as referee for one of Valentino's well-publicised 'work-outs' in the boxing-ring. Such pugilistic skills came in useful for challenging impertinent newspaper reporters if they bruised his more sensitive feelings

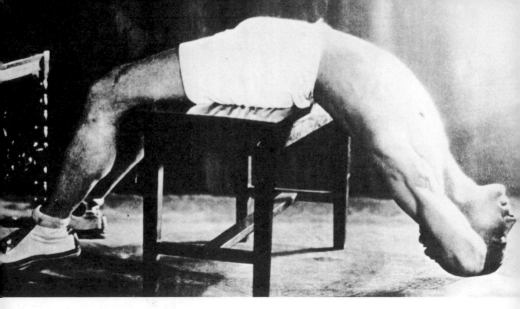

his artistry with gimcrack productions done without taste—and without Natacha. In this last deficiency lay the reason for the many displays of temper Lasky now had to endure. An emphasis on artistic 'integrity' frequently follows a sudden attack of stardom: it is the artist's way of keeping sane in the maelstrom of promotional events all seeming to suck his sense of personal identity out from him. Valentino was now going through this disorienting experience and at the same time he was finding the unfulfilled ambitions of Natacha Rambova were adding to the strain. Both of them had been upset when *Blood and Sand* had been made for economy reasons in the studio, rather than on location in Spain. They had imported many genuine Spanish artefacts, bought with money Lasky advanced, but somehow these didn't give them the authentic *frisson* of art, of being psychically in touch with the past, which they had decided the historical sites in Spain would have provided. Natacha at this stage had set her heart on moving on from designing Valentino's films to actually producing them—and Lasky knew how costly that would be. The feeling which the pair had that they were being 'exploited' was increased by the enviable example of Douglas Fairbanks Sr right there in the home acre. Fairbanks had been his own producer and star, and his own distributor as well with the formation of United Artists in 1919; and his mammoth production of *Robin Hood*, which was designed around his athletic *braggadocio*, combined exactly the kind of costume spectacle and commercial success that Valentino and Natacha envied and wished to emulate—though theirs would of course be much more 'artistic'. One senses a desire to provoke a breach with Lasky.

For his next film, though, Valentino insisted on a story that Lasky felt did him little justice and might do even less for the company's profits. *The Young Rajah* was not even a favourite with Valentino: it was a low-keyed modern story about a young American at Harvard

Valentino's obsession with physical fitness may have had its origins in the less-than-virile taunts that jealous males addressed to the 'Great Lover'

Valentino and Natacha photographed like royal personages ready for their imprimatur on stamp or coin. In profile, they were remarkably similar, even down to the smooth glossiness of their preferred hair-style. The degree of their composure is also noteworthy: there are very few pictures of either that betray the slightest discomposure with their lot or the world in general

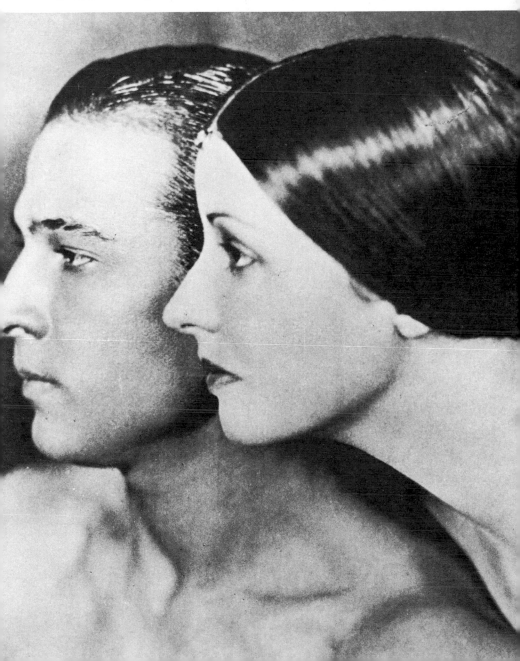

who turns out to be the son of the Maharajah of Dharmagar and returns to India to overcome a usurper and marry his college girl. But June Mathis had found the story and written the script. He trusted her advice. And what both of them found intriguing were the story's supernatural elements: the hero had extra-sensory powers; he was warned in visions about impending doom (usually prefaced by a glowing spot on his temples); he experienced prophetic dreams; and when he assumes the trappings of his Indian heritage, he is 'reincarnated', as it were, into a more exotic body than that of a Harvard man. As it turned out, Valentino's dramatic judgment was sounder than his spiritualist sympathies. *The Young Rajah* was hardly what the public expected. His performance has slowed down to the pace of a sleep-walking trance filled with little starts of prophetic apprehension and still further interrupted by boding titles hinting that man is a spiritual embryo who must fulfil his destiny or perish. Even though he holds a girl in his arms with the old tenderness, the intensity he is forced to mime when afflicted with his spiritual migraine suggests that the vision in front of him is not his beloved, but his troubled future. Natacha's design which she forwarded to Hollywood from New York, where she was prudently waiting out the interlocutory decree, turned the oriental scenes into a masque that was impressive but static. The reviews were poor, though the public were drawn by the novelty of seeing Valentino as a Hindu in bangles and jewels reclining languidly on a swan-boat barge.

By the time the film was released, late in 1922, Valentino and his studio were at legal loggerheads. He had joined Natacha in New York, unassuaged by Lasky's parting gift of a bag of gold-plated golf-clubs, and it must be assumed that her pent-up resentment at being 'exiled' from his side in Hollywood now worked on his own distempered mood to provoke an open breach. 'I cannot work for this motion picture corporation,' he charged publicly. 'I cannot endure the tyranny, the broken promises, the arrogance or the system of production. I cannot forgive the cruelty of the company to Mrs Valentino.' Lasky responded with an injunction compelling Valentino either to honour his contract, which ran until 1924, or forgo appearances for anyone else

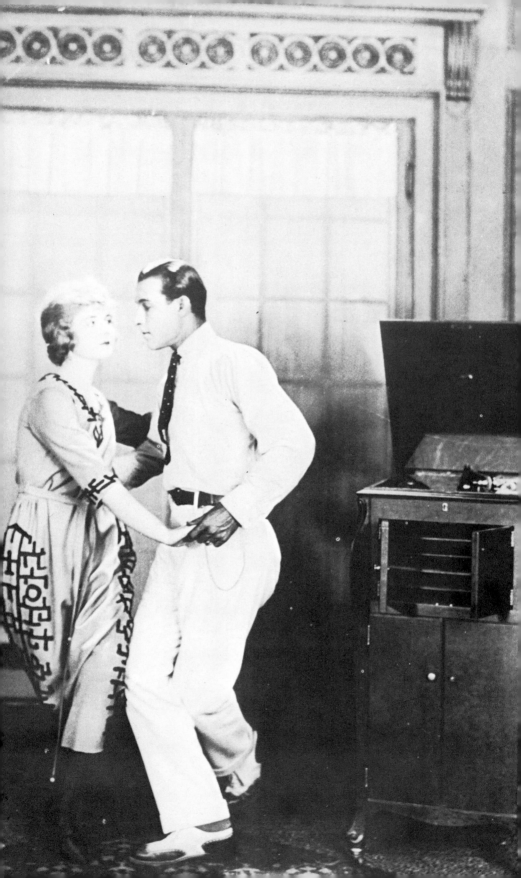

'either in pictures or on the speaking stage.' Soon star and studio were in a state of mutual siege on opposite sides of America. The studio offered enormous financial inducements—a huge rise to $7,000 weekly—but the star wouldn't abate his demands for artistic control. Over the next few months he lived on the only capital he had amassed—the public's adulation and interest in his least movement. He collaborated on a highly fanciful autobiography and put his name to *Day Dreams*, a volume of swooning poetry said to have been inspired by psychic communication with contributors who were designated by their initials only: 'R.B.' for Robert Browning, 'W.W.' for Walt Whitman and 'G.S.' for George Sand, though some of the more vulgar fans assumed this was Gloria Swanson. He even did a radio broadcast a few days before Christmas 1922, devoted to 'The Truth About Myself', though most of it dealt with 'the truth', as Valentino saw it, about the film industry whose product was 'a brazen insult to the public's intelligence'. Fighting words!

They must have rankled and anyhow they make it quite plausible that the studio, as Valentino alleged, now began disseminating stories

Valentino demonstrates the tango that made him famous. By now he is so confident that he can afford to spoof it a little

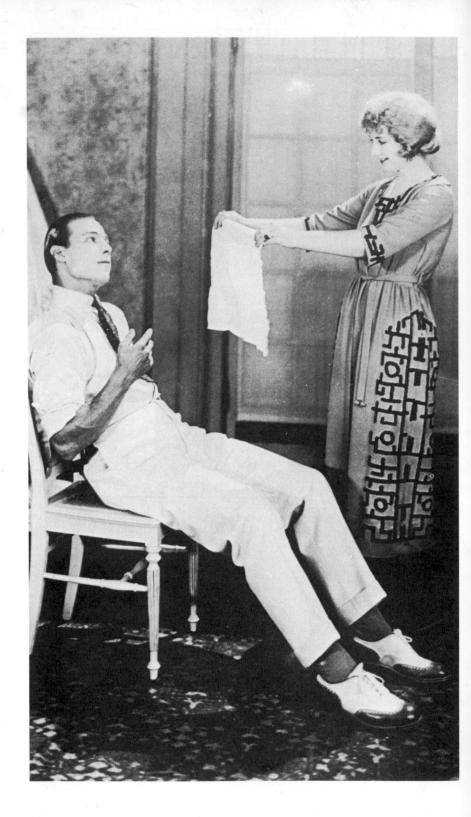

about his 'indolence, effeteness, and being under a woman's domination, leisurely reclining on downy sofas, supported by silken pillows and wickedly smoking sheikishly perfumed cigarettes.'

For all his bold front, it was an anxious period for Valentino. He owed Lasky some $70,000 and more debts were being accumulated daily as construction proceeded back in Hollywood on a palatial home for him and Natacha. A partial easing of their perilous solvency was found by their new public relations manager, George Ullman, whom they had hired after psychic inspiration. Ullman brought a more solid advantage when he arranged for them to tour America, for $7,000 weekly, in a private railroad car, publicising a face-cream product after they had gone through a routine of exotic dances. Then in mid-1923 Valentino was sued by his own lawyers for nearly $50,000. Money seems to have dictated a speedy settlement with Lasky, though the studio had been as impressed by the number and loyalty of Valentino's fans as the star had been impressed by the volume of his own debts. The settlement required him to make only two more films for Lasky, at a salary of $7,500 a week, with influence over the stories, co-stars and directors. And Natacha, with whom he had gone through a second marriage ceremony in March 1923, got control of the production design. It was quite a victory—and there was an ironical bonus. While Valentino had been kept legally off the screen in anyone else's films, the company had been feverishly capitalising on his well-publicised feud with them by re-releasing his recent films, so that he had been kept continuously before the public by the very enemy he was fighting.

Before embarking on his new film, *Monsieur Beaucaire*, Valentino made a grand tour of Europe and discovered how his popularity had escalated into international fame. Recognised in London wherever they went, he and Natacha dined with the Guinnesses at Ascot, lunched with Lord and Lady Birkenhead at the Savoy, met Gladys Cooper and Gerald Du Maurier, purchased three Pekes from exclusive kennels and, after a swift but expensive round of shopping, journeyed to Paris by air for more fêteing, adding a Dobermann Pinscher to the litter and ordering two custom-built Voisin tourers before descending on Valentino's brother Alberto and his sister Maria in Italy by way of the Hudnut château near Nice. Ironically enough, Italy was the one land where he went generally incognito, as his most recent movies hadn't penetrated very widely there. 'I was as I had been when I left,' he noted, 'as unknown to films as films were (then) unknown to me.' Mussolini couldn't find the time to meet him, though lunch with d'Annunzio provided consolation. To those who remembered him in his home town of Castellaneta, he was still a Guglielmi, a name that hadn't been much in the headlines. However, he was well content when he and Natacha sailed back to the United States in the autumn of 1923. A career stretched ahead of him that was now his to guide. He was at the height of his fame. His happiness seemed assured. He had also rather less than three years to live.

The home life of the most famous Italian in movies—not very different from that of millions of his countrymen, at least as far as cooking went. This is Valentino at his most relaxed

As Monsieur Beaucaire: Valentino at his most courtly

Leading Doris Kenyon in the dance and showing his customary physical finesse at drawing character out of the way he controlled and displayed his body

Routing the enemy in Monsieur Beaucaire

6

THE NEW FILM *Monsieur Beaucaire* was made
in the Paramount studios at Astoria, New York, so Natacha
Rambova's influence was stronger on every aspect of it than might
have been the case in Hollywood. It was designed as an 'art' picture
from first shot to last; and Valentino unselfishly subordinated himself
to his wife's concept at considerable risk to his own image. For nearly
half the film he sinks his customary appeal untraceably into the
portrait of a parasitic eighteenth-century courtier who lets women
insult his virility to his face and is taunted into flexing his muscles
only when he is the victim of an arranged marriage. Film-goers who
came expecting the swashbuckling brio of a Fairbanks got a shock
when they first saw Valentino as a wasp-waisted, limp-wristed beau
with *two* beauty spots on his cheek doing a stiffly elegant dance or
leaning languidly against the wings of the palace's toy theatre,
playing a lute of no doubt authentic but absurdly exaggerated
proportions. Valentino's levee is supposed to be a mockery of a
debilitated life-style, but it succeeds almost too well. The star stands
there waiting to be dressed by his servants, stripped to the waist and
flinging out his chest as if to ward off the contagion of pansiness from a
primping queen who takes out a vanity box to freshen his lipstick and
then delicately plucks his eyebrows. The fans must have wondered
what the sheik was doing in this *galère*. What's so admirable however is
the detailed consistency Valentino preserves in his foppish portrait.
He slides into each posture of artificiality and inbred langour as if he
were being painted by a court artist. He deploys his walking cane like a
spindly third limb on which he swivels with studied lassitude. He
develops a characterisation that differs *bodily*, as well as psychologi-
cally, from any of his earlier, more vigorous roles and he bears all
Sydney Olcott's tableauesque direction with the fortitude that was
probably essential in a French monarch's court where life, if the film is
to be believed, consisted of people being endlessly introduced to each
other.

When the beau runs off to England and masquerades as the French
Ambassador's barber, out-duelling, out-gambling and out-loving
all comers, the old Valentino comes out of hiding, though not without

Lunch-time in the commissary at Paramount's studios in Astoria, N.Y., during the shooting of Monsieur Beaucaire. *Valentino and Natacha in street clothes are at the table on the left*

The Valentinos off duty, but still setting fashion in lounge-wear. The photograph is inscribed 'To our dear Golden Girl . . .' This may have meant the screen-writer June Mathis or the medium who conducted the seances that were held in their Whitley Heights home

an ironic wink at his 'Great Lover's' persona. 'I was never so happy,' he soliloquizes, as he shaves his master. 'No one knows me. No one expects me to make love to them.' This release of energy must have refreshed his fans. Even so, the film's artistic pretensions delay its full display. The duel when Valentino first goes into action is suggested only by the tips of the rapiers lunging at and parrying each other while the umpire is 'irised' in the centre, watching the hits and awarding points to the unseen adversaries. Putting the 'vulgar' display of athletic activity completely out of sight is a concept that only a consciously 'artistic' talent like Natacha's would have engineered. But film-goers must have felt a bit hard done by, having to wait for the big sword-fight at the end in which Valentino at last lives up to their expectations. James R. Quirk, editor of the influential *Photoplay* magazine, put his finger on the reason why the film, for all its impressive production detail, failed to please the public as much as had been hoped. 'Rudy,' he wrote in the September issue,' is trying to be an actor at the expense of the personality that made him a sensation. . . . Except for one or two rattling good swordfights, the old spark disappears. He doesn't look a bit dangerous to women. The fact of the matter is that they like their Rudy a little wicked. He had what is known in pictures as 'menace' to a higher degree than any star on the screen. As Beaucaire, he has about as much of this quality as Charlie Chaplin.' Natacha, of course, hardly shared this view. 'Some of the farmers (peasants?) of God's Country had taken unkindly to the white wigs,' she sniffed.

The Valentinos' life together, outside working hours, was now apeing the sumptuousness that had been lavished on their film. They were seen at most of the important auctions of furniture and fine art in New York, snapping up costly bric-a-brac for use in future films or for decorating their California home. Cloth-of-gold scarves. French walnut chests, Arabic trays, illuminated vellums, Turkish coffee-services, suits of Moorish armour: as in her choice of scripts, Natacha abhorred anything modern. Ultimately a lot of these pieces had to be put into store, as they scarcely fitted the rather small dimensions of the Whitley Heights home which they had no sooner moved into than Natacha declared to be cramped and inappropriate to their status, despite such elaborate and almost regal touches as a *chaise percée* of ducal origin in the lavatory and a perfume vaporizer that wafted scent through Natacha's dressing room while she made her toilette.

Elephantiasis of the creative will appears to have overtaken them both in the wake of their victory over Lasky. As if to assert their authority, they ran up debt recklessly. One of those who came to their rescue was Joseph Schenck, head of United Artists which distributed the films of Fairbanks, Pickford, Chaplin and D. W. Griffith. Schenck had earlier put his hand into his pocket to bail Valentino out of jail following his marriage mix-up. It was a canny move, for United Artists needed more films to distribute than its founder-stars could provide and Schenck would have valued having Valentino contribute to their

During the feud with his studio, Valentino had a series of photos taken of him at home in Whitley Heights. They were used to promote the dancing tour with Natacha: they stress the self-absorption and loneliness of a star with time on his hands

production roster. Even more watchful of his chance to acquire the star's services, now that he had only one more film to make for Lasky, Schenck personally guaranteed the $175,000 asked for the new mansion, standing on a more commanding site in the Hollywood Hills, into which the Valentinos wished to move. It had stables, kennels, dog runs, garaging for four automobiles, a servants' wing and nearly ten acres of land. Valentino named it Falcon Lair and gave Natacha a free hand in decorating it, making only the stipulation that he should have a 'den' of his own.

When we look at the sexual image Valentino acquired off-screen, in his 'private' life, we find it extremely low-key. This may be surprising at first, for such is the power of stardom that the off-screen lives of those who have it seem to be recast in its image. With Valentino, it is definitely not so. He had no scandal following him around town where other women were concerned: his love-life is not only not lurid, but it scarcely exists. He was, of course, a married man right from the start of his public celebrity, with one wife following swiftly upon the divorce of another, even though there was that unconventional legal 'hiccup' in the procedure, and he had therefore to behave like a faithful lover, if not a 'great' one. All kinds of morality groups, lay and religious, were focusing their indignant sights on the lives led by the Hollywood stars. Although the place was like a small town in many of its attitudes, despite the great wealth that the inhabitants flaunted, it had been shaken by such scandals in the early 1920s as Fatty Arbuckle's manslaughter trials, Wallace Reid's death from drugs, and the murder of the director William Desmond Taylor. Any sex scandal involving Valentino would have been dynamite in this atmosphere: so he would have had every professional reason for keeping his 'Great Lover' image confined to the screen and not indulging it practically. Actually, this suited him for temperamental reasons, too. Valentino had a well-developed Italian liking for the well-run household, the comfortable domestic set-up where life was regulated by the women without the man having to trouble his head too much about it. Luigi Barzini refers to this as a propensity to *sistemare*, and it enabled Valentino to fall in line with Natacha's plans for him even more easily. She was boss.

92

Falcon Lair, the house Valentino bought for himself and Natacha, but which he alone occupied. The pennant over the entrance features an embroidered 'V'

Inside Falcon Lair, furnished in the Spanish style with many of the antiques bought by the Valentinos on their tours of Europe. The large portrait of the master as a Spanish gentleman is the work of the then fashionable artist Beltran y Masses

All the appurtenances of stardom—and heavy bank overdrafts—
surrounded Valentino at Falcon Lair. He had a stable of
thoroughbreds . . .

. . . expensive motor-cars custom-built for him in Europe,
including this tourer with the coiled snake on the bonnet, a
symbol of good luck . . .

. . . a kennel of dogs contributed to the aristocratic elegance

Valentino kept himself—and his legend—in shape with the strenuous life expected of a film star . . . fencing . . . yachting . . . polo playing

Reporters noticed that from this time on he began sporting the platinum slave bracelet she had designed for him—rather imprudently, he told them he also had a gold one for night wear. Neither Valentino nor his wife appears to have experienced any deep sexual need for each other. She would certainly have considered a family to be a serious block to a career. Her memoirs contain not one reference to any sexual intimacies, which is surprising considering that she was, after all, married to the screen's 'Great Lover'. If he pressed his sexual attentions on her, she could hardly say that she had repulsed them without raising awkward questions about her own sexuality. But the point is that she makes no mention of them. For Natacha, Valentino remained essentially 'a child' who loved new things—cameras became one of his crazes as the age of the portable 'candid' camera came in. He could 'make you see wonders in anything in which he was interested at the moment.' For relaxation away from Natacha, he turned to his constant circle of bachelor friends, actors, photographers, a director or two, some of them certainly homosexual. Natacha often mocked their all-male get-togethers; but as young women, whether established stars or raw beginners, were hardly part of this group's interests, she had no other cause for offence. There is only one reference made by Valentino to any possible sexual dissatisfaction with his marriage. 'A man may admire a woman without desiring her,' he said to an interviewer. 'He may respect the brilliance of her mind, the nobility of her character, yes, even the beauty of her face and body, yet she may not move him emotionally.' It has been reported that Natacha construed this as a veiled reference to her Lesbianism and, on reading it, slapped Valentino's face. But such a report is necessarily hard to confirm.

What is clear is that from mid-1924 until their separation Natacha's insistence on ordering her husband's career met with more and more opposition from studio executives and also with increasing vexation on the part of Valentino himself. Lasky had followed *Monsieur Beaucaire* with the last of his contract films, *A Sainted Devil*. This was a deliberate return to his fan-pleasing style as a hot-blooded South American. But the emotional tone of his performance is far darker than in *The Four Horsemen of the Apocalypse*. He excels in scenes which show a man driven to drink and remorse. He found these were very much to his liking, a *machismo* emotion that other, later stars would strive to experience as an earnest of their Hollywood integrity—as if pain somehow verified their existence. Natacha supervised the film closely—so closely, in fact, that she had Jetta Goudal, one of the co-stars, dismissed from the production for slighting her costume designs. (Unkind tongues put it around that she also thought Miss Goudal had been altogether too familiar with Valentino when not vamping him on screen). When the film was finished Valentino and Lasky parted company with protestations of mutual affection. Lasky instantly tried to replace him with Ricardo Cortez. And Irving

Care was taken to design a frame that enhanced the romantic
allure of the star whether he was in costume with a woman, as in
A Sainted Devil *and* The Eagle, *or alone in a business suit in*
Cobra, *overleaf, his only film in which someone else got the girl*

Shulman quotes other studio executives as congratulating themselves on getting rid of 'a double hernia'.

The Valentinos now started on the contract they had entered into with Ritz-Carlton Productions, which had promised them control over the productions and a share of the profits. The first film they planned was *The Scarlet Power* (later renamed *The Hooded Falcon*), essentially the El Cid story for which Natacha now wrote a treatment, leaving it to the ever faithful June Mathis to do the shooting script, and in the late summer of 1924 she and her husband sailed for Europe to spend $100,000 of Ritz-Carlton's money on collecting period artefacts for the movie. But on their return they found that June Mathis's as yet incomplete screenplay would cost many more dollars than could be sanctioned by Ritz-Carlton, who were learning fast about the price of their new stars. Natacha took the blow badly and disdained the offer to design the stop-gap production that Valentino committed himself to make while the other script was being pared down to size and budget. This was the film version of a stage hit called *Cobra*. 'A modern story,' sneered Natacha, her head still filled with the medieval glories of El Cid. Valentino was cast as an impoverished Italian nobleman working for a New York antique dealer. It was the first film in which he didn't get the girl at the end—he nobly surrendered her to the dealer—and the only one of his major movies in which he played one of his own countrymen. It is an impeccably dressed production: one feels all those shopping sprees being used to effect in the antique-shop scenes. And it had the familiar 'flashback' sequence where the characters 'return' to be their own ancestors in an earlier century. Valentino's renunciation scene, sacrificing his own true love to his friend's happiness, emphasised the maturer range of emotion he could express; and there is a loneliness and pessimism in his characterisation that may be reflecting the disenchantment setting in with his marriage.

Natacha and he were bitterly disappointed to be told, early in 1925, that the film company would not proceed with *The Hooded Falcon*. Though Natacha had had no hand in designing *Cobra*, she had interfered on all levels and the company feared what letting her rip on a costume epic could cost in terms of ego and extravagance. She had cherished this film above all other projects, believing it would conclusively exalt her taste and her husband's talent to the level of acknowledged art. To have it abruptly cancelled brought her up against a reality she had not previously encountered—the possibility that Valentino's fame might be mortal, his power limited. From this event dates the swiftly widening breach in their marriage. Valentino's services were instantly acquired by Joseph Schenck of United Artists, for $10,000 weekly, three films a year, and up to forty-two per cent of the net profits—a deal that put him on a financial level with the highest paid stars of the day. But the same contract that enhanced him brutally demoted Natacha, completely stripping her of any say in his pictures and even banning her from visiting the shooting stages. A

Consternation was caused—at least to the master barbers of America—when Valentino returned from a trip to Europe wearing a beard and moustache. He was persuaded to shave them off . . . but not before making costume tests for the film for which he grew them, a version of the El Cid story to be called The Hooded Falcon. *The film was never made*

For Valentino, there was at least the compensation of being able to wear a beard for the historical flashback sequence in his next film, Cobra

In all other respects, Cobra *portrayed a thoroughly modern Valentino whose pursuit of the girl (Gertrude Olmstead) was one of impeccable gallantry—only this time, he failed to win her hand*

marriage that was based on a mutuality of professional admiration could not possibly survive this shock. Valentino was already so deeply into debt with Schenck that he could hardly have afforded *not* to sign the contract: but Natacha scornfully accused him of selling out for money. It was something that 'artists' did not do! She would hear nothing about his work from now on, even forbade any mention of his new film, *The Eagle*, in her presence and refused to move into the newly furnished Falcon Lair. Out of guilt and remorse, Valentino agreed to finance an independent production for his wife, a satire called *What Price Beauty?* But out of prudence, he limited the budget to $25,000.

In mid-August 1925, Valentino with a large retinue of Pressmen and photographers saw his wife off on the train to New York where she was ostensibly going to try and arrange the release of her new film. (It had gone over budget and was having trouble finding a distributor.) Both were as faultlessly dressed as ever, she in a turban and white summer gloves with a heavily embroidered calf-length dress that lent her a medieval stateliness, he in impeccable blazer and flannels and white fedora, his 'co-respondent' shoes twinkling as brightly in the sunshine as the Isotta-Fraschini in which they had motored to Pasadena. Like any loving husband seeing his wife off on a short journey, Valentino assisted Natacha up the little steps and into her Pullman drawing-room. Appearances were preserved to the end. But it was the last occasion that the pair were pictured together as a married couple and the last time Valentino was ever to see his wife.

Shortly after her arrival in New York, Natacha was telling reporters, 'When a husband and wife both are working and both are the possessors of temperaments, I think they should have a vacation from each other. Since I've been making my own pictures we have been drawn more or less apart, and I can't find the time to devote to the home that I used to.' As an afterthought, which some considered a spiteful little jab at the 'Great Lover' she had married, she added, 'My husband is a great lover of home life.' Statement followed statement as news of the separation became official. Valentino at the urging of Schenck at first maintained a dignified sadness of the 'best of friends' variety—'I am sorry this had to happen, but we cannot always order our lives the way we would like to have them.' Natacha on the other hand grew more and more snappish. Announcing her intention to follow an independent acting career she told reporters, 'I won't sit and twiddle my fingers, waiting for a husband who goes on the lot at 5.00 a.m. and gets home at midnight, and receives mail from girls in Oshkosh and Kalamazoo.' Valentino retorted, 'Mrs Valentino cannot have a career and be my wife at the same time.' And at the beginning of November 1925, as he was entraining for the New York première of *The Eagle*, he was even more abrupt: 'You know, I am just beginning to feel that I was as well off single as I was married.'

The Eagle, directed by Clarence Brown, won Valentino the immediate applause of fans and critics: it was his 'comeback' film, and, in

Valentino sees his wife off on the train. To spectators, it may have looked a devoted and temporary parting—and both, as usual, never let appearances betray their inner thoughts—but in fact it was to be their final separation. Neither saw the other again

Variety's words, what he had come back to was 'the he-man stuff'. He played a romantic and athletic sort of Russian Robin Hood who catches a runaway coach containing Vilma Banky at the start of the film with a piece of muscular bravado worthy of Fairbanks. His virility is once again frankly on display. So is his hint of cruelty. Disguised as 'The Eagle', he abducts Vilma and looks her up and down with *droit-de-seigneur* coldness as he casts a meaningful glance at his horse whip. Then a boyish gleam of frank delight thaws his face as the title comes up: 'Milady, you are as beautiful as you are free—and that is very, very free.' His sense of humour is shared with film-goers in scenes like the one where Louise Dresser's stoutly corseted Empress Catherine closes her eyes as she utters some Imperial endearment over the kneeling Valentino. With a puckish glint in his eye, Valentino sidles silently out from under the hand that's poised to pat his head and leaves the Empress stroking the empty air for a second or two before she realises the object of her pursuit is no longer there. Valentino's movements are as finely tuned as ever to some inner tempo. When he mimes his sorrow at his father's deathbed, his hand hovers a millimetre over his temples—and the dying man need not be there, so gently does the gesture express his presence. Valentino once more looks in tip-top physical form after the rather constipated passivity of Beaucaire. His strength is like a ballet dancer's, accustomed to lifting a woman from ground to horseback in one effortless hoist. His steely body control, his fine bones and the sudden elasticity of his face remind one of Jean-Louis Barrault when he played the mime Baptiste in *Les Enfants du Paradis*.

A day or two after the film's New York opening Valentino applied for American citizenship, then boarded the liner *Leviathan* for France where he intended to establish domicile for the purpose of his divorce. Natacha had arrived back off the same liner from France, where she had gone for the same purpose. Far from the volleys of vituperative charges having hurt Valentino's stardom, they had made him into an even more fascinating celebrity to his public. For being 'free' of one woman, particularly someone supposed to have altogether too possessive a hold on him, meant he 'belonged' even more legitimately

About to give the slip to the pursuing charms of Louise Dresser's Empress of Russia in The Eagle

In The Eagle, *one of his most stylish and vigorous performances*

to his admirers. Any woman who could catch his eye could now fancy she ran the risk of a seduction; and speculation was intense about who his next real-life love would be. Without suggesting his professional interest in women was any the less, Valentino teasingly made a wager with his public by taking a vow on New Year's Eve 1926, that he would '... never marry again. I backed up my pledge by accepting a five-to-one bet of $10,000 that I will still be unmarried in 1930. The bet is registered at the Sporting Club de Monte Carlo.' Natacha was also quoted as declaring that she had 'no intention of marrying again'. She didn't introduce any sporting risk into her pledge.

Valentino's bachelor status hadn't abated his extravagance. Quite the reverse. His spirits lifted so swiftly after the separation that he embarked on a highly publicised and therefore costly social life of a kind he had never had the encouragement to lead when evenings were spent at home with his wife in Whitley Heights going over ever more audacious plans for their great 'art' films. It was undoubtedly a response that caused concern to his friends as he drew improvidently on his already depleted bank account and brushed aside George Ullman's warning of impending bankruptcy. When faced with the imminent likelihood of this, he made a determined attempt to recoup his solvency with one blow—he turned back to the role that had given him stardom and clinched his image and announced that his next film would be a sequel to *The Sheik*.

The Son of the Sheik, as it was called, was based on Edith Hull's own sequel entitled *The Sons of the Sheik* though the two 'sons' became 'one' for the film so as to concentrate attention on the star. Valentino, however, decided to play his own father in the film, as an extra element of box-office appeal. The film shows the extreme extent to which love, hate and masochism were now accepted parts of Valentino's persona. He was a romantic star who could be killed off at the end of a film without disenchanting the fans. They felt that his romantic pact was with death, not with some competitive blonde or brunette, and this same sense of renunciation was to hover round his death-bed in New York only a few months later. He had died for his country in *The Four Horsemen of the Apocalypse* and for his honour in *Blood and Sand* where his gored body is dragged out of the bullring leaving a trail of blood that is sanded over for the next sacrifice of man or beast. He had developed a strong predilection for suffering, as we have seen, and *The Son of the Sheik* serves this well in the torture scenes when the sheik is captured by his enemies, strung up by the arms and whipped. The film was an immense advance on *The Sheik* not only in direction—he had at last got George Fitzmaurice who had been replaced by Fred Niblo on *Blood and Sand* much to Valentino's annoyance—but also in the area of erotic psychology. For this sheik's actions in abducting a dancing girl are motivated not by love, but by hatred and revenge. Most of the film is concerned with a man's desire to even the score with a girl he suspects has played him false. The elements of menace and brutality

*Strung up and ready
to be scourged in
Son of the Sheik.
Pain and hatred were
built into the role and
welcomed by Valentino
as corresponding to
his mood after the
separation from
Natacha*

are exploited vividly in virtually every expression Valentino wears during the forceful seduction of Vilma Banky. Their previous love-making has been more erotic, too, with Valentino extending his kissing all along the girl's arm and shoulder—the days of cheeky interest in a woman's palm were over.

Once he has abducted her, he wrenches her suppliant arms away from him and forces her down on to the divan in his tent, his eyes shadowed and coldly vengeful. The sheik lights up a cigarette—a family habit it would seem—strips off his robe and unclasps his bejewelled belt. The girl's fear is clearly mingled with desire, a bold combination in the days before Miss Blandish's equivocal experience had become popular knowledge. 'I may not be the first victim,' he cries, 'but, by Allah, I'll be the one you remember!' Then with muscles bulging like a blacksmith shaping up to the anvil, he declaims, 'An eye for an eye, a hate for a hate' and spurns her like a dog as she clings pleadingly to his legs. The camera now assumes Valentino's subjective view of the cringing Vilma as he advances on her into a giant close-up of her dilated eyes: a very effective shot. He seizes her and crushes her lips with kisses. The camera reveals a bed. And like a sheep-dog cornering a fearful stray, Valentino drives the girl backwards towards it. . . . Fitzmaurice used a wind machine generously and the tent's fluttering draperies embody the fear of the sequence in a way that the tableauesque stances of the earlier film never could. The character's obsessive misogyny ('All the beauties of the Arabian Nights being unveiled could not get a look from me') suggests a purgative zeal that may have been provoked by the breach with Natacha. Valentino had approached the role more as a duty than a prospective delight, out of a need to make money quickly, not stretch his talents. But once in it, the psychological drives of the young sheik connected with his own embittered disposition. *The Son of the Sheik* with its insistent sado-eroticism took the 'Latin Lover' concept to the perverse extreme. It was a deliberate calculation of where the fans' gratification was to be found. And the result was a film that, being generally released throughout America a few weeks after Valentino's death, had the definitive quality of an obituary notice and played a major part in the necrophilia that followed him to the grave.

7

It was on 15 August, a stiflingly hot Sunday, when Valentino was rushed to the Polyclinic hospital in New York. He had gone to the city for the film's première on the East Coast. That evening he underwent surgery for a gastric ulcer and a ruptured appendix. Rumours began to spread almost immediately, however, that his sudden illness was due to nothing of the sort, and they intensified when it was learned that he had been taken ill, clutching at his stomach and falling on the carpet in agony, at a private party given by a young stockbroker friend of his the night before, at which were various showgirls. The suspicion was that an 'orgy' had been taking place; later on it would be asserted that Valentino had been poisoned by friends of Bianca De Saulles' late husband; and there was even a report that he had been shot by a jealous husband. The sudden illness of film stars, at the height of their celebrity, invariably releases just such a spate of myth-making rumours. The deaths of James Dean and Bruce Lee are other examples. Valentino's brother Alberto, who was in Europe at the time and did not get back to New York till after his death, was later offered an autopsy, but refused it, saying 'At that stage, what would one have found?' What *is* probable is that Valentino's ulcerated state hadn't been helped by the aggravation he had suffered some days previously in Chicago where the *Tribune* had printed the insulting imputation that he had debauched American manhood by the 'unmasculine' image he had popularised, the proof of which the *Tribune* found in a machine in a men's room that dispensed pink face powder if a powder puff was held under its nozzle. *Time* magazine reported that Valentino read the editorial in a rapidly mounting fury over breakfast while 'his thick wrists tinkled with a perpetual *arpeggio* of fine gold bangles'. He immediately staged a boxing bout with a sparring partner for the benefit of the Press, to demonstrate his virility, and challenged the anonymous author of 'the effusion' to stand up to him in the ring. There were no takers.

The public interest in the ailing star, as his condition weakened with the unexpected onset of peritonitis, a painful inflammation of the gall bladder, was unprecedented. Previously only the deaths of presidents or monarchs had aroused such a nation-wide response. Not that it was

An admirer—a woman, naturally—pauses before the open casket containing Valentino. She was one of over 100,000 people who filed past the catafalque in New York City

The scene outside Campbell's funeral parlour, where crowds waited in line for hours

entirely spontaneous. One reason for the phenomenon was the arrival of radio as a constant feature of the urban media. To have a movie hero, the 'Great Lover' of the screen, actually dying on one's doorstep was a gift for the New York and the out-of-town broadcasters who continuously informed hundreds of thousands of listeners about the stricken star's daily condition and generated a far more emotional effect by virtue of the urgency or anxiety in their voices than cold print could have done. Not that the 'cold print' was exactly frozen with grief. There was a fierce circulation war going on amongst New York's various tabloids at just this time; and as each tried to scoop the other with 'inside exclusives' (one of which was a faked photo of Valentino in the operating theatre) the star's plight took on the dimensions of a national catastrophe. All through Sunday, 22 August, Valentino's condition worsened and early the next morning, rambling deliriously in French and Italian, he received extreme unction. Shortly after the hour of noon, he died. He was aged thirty-one.

There followed the most remarkable and riotous lying-in-state ever witnessed in New York City. As radio stations hourly broadcast the wave of shock sweeping across the world, and the newspapers greeted his demise as a gift to their contentious circulation tactics, one of them even going so far as to use a 'photograph' of the star being received in Heaven by none other than Caruso, crowds started collecting outside the funeral parlour where Valentino lay in a half-open casket, his hair slicked down into the familiar patent-leather imitation of life, his eyebrows freshly pencilled by a make-up man and his cheeks rouged in a manner that did indeed recall the gibe about the 'pink powder-puff'. Incited by the publicity, the crowds turned into a mob which had to be beaten back by mounted police. Over a hundred people were injured. By the time the funeral parlour closed its doors a few days later, over 100,000 people had filed past the catafalque on which lay a profusion of floral tributes including an eleven-foot by six-foot pall of 4,000 scarlet roses sent ahead by Pola Negri who was herself hastening across the Continent by train, sporting a $3,000 mourning outfit and swooning with exclamations of grief and declarations of eternal love for the dead Valentino whose name had been romantically linked with hers only a few short weeks ago. The publicity of stardom was built into even the ceremonies of death. The funeral service took place in New York on 30 August attended by many Hollywood figures as well as Jean Acker, Natacha Rambova's half-sister (Natacha was in Paris and had uttered not a word during the illness) and Joseph Schenck, whose grief at his contract artist's death must have been lightened by the insurance policies he had prudently taken out on his life as well as by the swelling receipts that *The Son of the Sheik* and *The Eagle* were continuing to bring in throughout America. As the service began at St Malachy's, the work going on in every film studio and on location 3,000 miles away in California came to a halt for two minutes. It was, perhaps, the tribute that Valentino would have valued most.

Valentino's coffin on its final journey. Among the honorary pallbearers are Douglas Fairbanks Sr, Adolph Zukor, head of Paramount, Marcus Loew, the theatre magnate, and Joseph Schenck, chief of United Artists for whom the actor made his last two films. They were playing to record audiences as the star was being buried, a fact that proved to Hollywood that good business was not impaired by bereavement. Summoned by the mass coverage of radio and Press, the crowds watching the funeral motorcade were record ones, too

His Will divided his estate equally between his brother and sister and a Mrs Theresa Werner who was Natacha Rambova's aunt and who had tried to repair the broken marriage. Of Jean Acker there was no mention. Natacha was cut off with the legacy of a single dollar.

For a long time it looked uncertain whether *anyone* would get more than a dollar out of the estate. Valentino died deeply in debt and Federal tax-claims kept on arriving over the weeks as Ullman, who had been named executor, tried to salvage the actor's assets. It took six days to auction Valentino's personal effects, some 2,036 items, but they made a disappointing total of under $100,000. His two houses, Falcon Lair and the Whitley Heights home referred to as 'The Temple of Love' in the auctioneer's advertisements, did little better. Valentino had been $160,000 in debt at his death and litigation over the Will, which dragged on unbelievably till 1947, drained even Ullman's reserves of energy, never mind cash. And yet by the 1930s there was a surplus on paper of nearly $800,000, much of it coming from the continuing box-office success of Valentino's re-issued movies in the last couple of which he had owned a substantial percentage. His earthly remains had been taken to Hollywood and placed, temporarily, in the family crypt of the woman to whom he owed his chance of stardom, June Mathis. But she died less than a year later and since the suitably resplendent mausoleum planned for Valentino had not yet been built—it was, in fact, the subject of a law suit—his casket was moved into June Mathis's husband's niche. There it remains, the object of annual and sometimes rowdy pilgrimage as his legend has drawn all kinds and classes of devotees on the anniversary of his death.

What would he have become had he lived? Shortly before his death he had told his brother that he had no plans to re-marry, at least while he was a star. If he did so eventually, it would not be to another actress, nor to anyone in the film business. It placed too great a strain on each of the parties. (Natacha Rambova, incidentally, married a Spanish nobleman in 1934 from whom she was later divorced. She died in California in 1966, almost seventy). After five years, Valentino felt, his fame as a leading man would be on the wane, along with his looks, and he planned to switch from acting in films to directing and producing them.

The unsatisfied curiosity one feels about Valentino's possible fate in the talkie revolution and the establishment of the studio system, which effectively clipped the wings as well as the salaries of the stars in the 1930s, has to be balanced against the gratification of seeing a phenomenon fulfil himself and leave the scene while he was still in possession of all his fame and power. One has to conclude, unsentimentally, that it was perhaps a good time for him to go. He had revealed the excitement of love-making to American womanhood: but women were already beginning to turn away from the exotic foreign model and back to the staple American product represented by a new star like John Gilbert. Valentino's frank revelling in his own sexuality on screen had affected the American male, too, and Gilbert generously acknowledged the style that the earlier star had set which enabled the new breed of Hollywood lover to play the ardent lover without embarrassment and in a way that restored to the ordinary film-goer his confidence in a romantic attitude that he had previously mocked through mistrust or jealousy. As for the ordinary film-goer's wife, she probably found it refreshing, too, to rediscover in her husband or, at any rate, in a more accessible type of screen lover personified by John Gilbert or Ronald Colman and later on by Clark Gable, all the flattering attentions, and sometimes that exciting little jag of male chauvinism, that had once seemed only to accompany a Latin name.

That Valentino had little luck in his own love life is something that posterity has chosen to ignore, if it is even aware of it. His name and image, *these* are the things that make him recognised and remembered. He left no diaries that reveal his sexual propensities; and the accounts of his friends are either unrevealing or untrustworthy on that score. As I have already remarked, his second wife omitted *them* from her memoirs as completely as his first wife had excluded *him* from her bedroom. The obvious pleasure he sought from the company of young men, often as handsome as himself, should not necessarily make us suppose he was homosexual. The films of Lattuada and Fellini, just to name a few sources, remind us that hanging around with the males in the gang, particularly if there was nothing else to do in a dead-end town, was part of the normal growing-up process for Italian youths and hadn't any ostensibly sexual aspect. Valentino never quite grew up—and never lost the need for 'the gang'. But the evidence also shows that he was no womaniser, either, except on the screen. He probably had as much of the suppressed bisexuality that is not infrequently found in the male Hollywood star who has to preserve a conventional attitude to sex in his public life while the image the films project of him, and the experience he has in the image-making machine called Hollywood, convert him, if need be, to a far less rigidly categorised view of gender. There is always something inherently feminine in the 'Great Lover', for it is his own narcissistic reflection he seeks in the depths of his beloved's eyes. Valentino's great talent lay in the completely natural way he was able to humanise this mythical figure in terms of his own sexuality—and if the latter quality contains a strong element of sexual ambiguity, this is not something that should entirely surprise us. Nor, on the evidence available, is it something we can confidently label.

Valentino focused an emotional need shared by millions at a particular time in history and he was fortunate in finding the right role that magnified his qualities and invited participation in the myth of love as he expressed it. For someone with so romantic an image, however, he was astutely practical in his approach to love in the movies. He appealed by his looks, he proved himself by his techniques, and he invested his interpretation with the sense of an ideal expressed in his smallest gestures and in his whole physical personality. Those looks, those techniques, those gestures, that personality may now be out of fashion, just as that ideal of love has been secularised today into the fact of sex. We have lost the power to believe in them: perhaps we never shall again. Valentino remains the timeless evidence that people did *once* believe in them. What he preserves for us is not just his own artistry: it is also our sense of wonder at all he stood for.

For many years after his death, Valentino's best-known mourner was the mysterious 'Lady in Black', who would appear on each anniversary in the burial crypt bearing roses

Filmography

VALENTINO PLAYED MINOR roles in a number of films released between 1918 and 1920. There is some doubt about the order in which he made them, but the general pattern appears to be as follows:

1918. Alimony. A Society Sensation. All Night.
1919. A Delicious Little Devil. A Rogue's Romance. The Homebreaker. Virtuous Sinners. The Big Little Person. Out of Luck. Eyes of Youth.
1920. The Married Virgin. An Adventuress. The Cheater. Passion's Playground. Once to Every Woman. Stolen Moments. The Wonderful Chance.

Major Films

The Four Horsemen of the Apocalypse, Metro: Eleven reels, premièred 6 March 1921. Rex Ingram (Director); June Mathis (Adapter); John F. Seitz (Photographer); Starrett Ford, Walter Mayo (Assistant Photographers); Joseph Calder, Amos Myers (Assistant Directors); Grant Whytock (Editor); Louis F. Gottschalk (Music); Walter Mayo (Art Director); Jack W. Robson (Art Titler); Rudolph Valentino (Julio Desnoyers), Alice Terry (Marguerite Laurier), Pomeroy Cannon (The Centaur), Joseph Swickard (Marcelo Desnoyers), Alan Hale (Karl von Hartrott), Nigel de Brulier (Tchernoff), Bridgetta Clark (Doña Luisa), Mabel van Buren (Elena) (Leading Players). Adapted from the novel *The Four Horsemen of the Apocalypse* by Blasco-Ibáñez (1918).

Uncharted Seas, Metro: Six reels, premièred 25 April 1921. Wesley Ruggles (Director); George Edward Jenks (Screenwriter); John F. Seitz (Photographer); John Holden (Art Director); Alice Lake (Lucretia Eastman), Carl Gerard (Sen. Eastman), Rudolph Valentino (Frank Underwood) (Leading Players). Based on 'The Uncharted Seas' by John Henry Wilson, published in *Munsey's Magazine*, September 1920.

Camille, Nazimova Productions; Metro: 5,600 feet, premièred 26 September 1921. Ray C. Smallwood (Director); June Mathis (Screenwriter-Adapter); Rudolph Bergquist (Photographer); Natacha Rambova (Art Director); Nazimova (Camille), Rudolph Valentino (Armand) (Leading Players). Adapted from the novel and the play *La Dame aux Camélias* by Alexandre Dumas (1848 and 1852).

The Conquering Power, Metro: Seven reels, premièred 8 July 1921. Rex Ingram (Producer-Director); June Mathis (Adapter); John F. Seitz (Photographer); Alice Terry (Eugénie Grandet), Rudolph Valentino (Charles Grandet), Eric Mayne (Victor Grandet), Ralph Lewis (Père Grandet) (Leading Players). Adapted from Balzac's novel *Eugénie Grandet* (1883).

The Sheik, Famous Players-Lasky, Paramount: 6,079 feet, premièred 30 October 1921. George Melford (Director); Monte Katterjohn (Screen-writer); William Marshall (Photographer); Agnes Ayres (Lady Diana), Rudolph Valentino (Sheik Ahmed Ben Hassan), Adolphe Menjou (Raoul de St. Hubert), Walter Long (Omair) (Leading Players). Adapted from Edith Maude Hull's novel *The Sheik* (1919).

Moran of the Lady Letty, Famous Players-Lasky, Paramount: 6,360 feet, premièred 12 February 1922. George Melford (Director); Monte Katterjohn (Adapter); William Marshall (Photographer); Dorothy Dalton (Moran), Rudolph Valentino (Ramon Laredo), Charles Brinley (Captain Sternersen), Walter Long (Captain Kitchell) (Leading Players). Adapted from Frank Norris's novel *Moran of the Lady Letty* (1898).

Beyond the Rocks, Famous Players-Lasky, Paramount: 6,740 feet, premièred 7 May 1922. Sam Wood (Director); Jack Cunningham (Adapter); Alfred Gilks (Photographer); Gloria Swanson (Theodora Fitzgerald), Rudolph Valentino (Lord Bracondale), Edythe Chapman (Lady Bracondale), Alec B. Tranis (Captain Fitzgerald) (Leading Players). Adapted from Elinor Glyn's novel *Beyond the Rocks* (1906).

Blood and Sand, Famous Players-Lasky, Paramount: 8,110 feet, pre-mièred 5 August 1922. Fred Niblo (Director); June Mathis (Screen-writer); Alvin Wyckoff (Photographer); Rudolph Valentino (Juan Gallardo), Lila Lee (Carmen), Nita Naldi (Doña Sol), George Field (El Nacional), Walter Long (Plumitas) (Leading Players). Adapted from the Blasco-Ibañez novel *Blood and Sand* (1908).

The Young Rajah, Famous Players-Lasky, Paramount: 7,708 feet, premièred 12 November 1922. Philip Rosen (Director); June Mathis (Adapter-Screenwriter); James C. Van Trees (Photographer); Rudolph Valentino (Amos Judd), Wanda Hawley (Molly Cabot), Jack Giddings (Austin Slade), Joseph Swickard (Narada) (Leading Players). Adapted from John Ames Mitchell's novel *Amos Judd* (1919).

Monsieur Beaucaire, Famous Players-Lasky, Paramount: 9,932 feet, premièred 18 August, 1924. Sidney Olcott (Director); Forrest Halsey (Screenwriter); Harry Fischbeck (Photographer); Natacha Rambova (Art Director); Patricia Rooney (Editor); Rudolph Valentino (Duc de Chartres/Beaucaire), Bebe Daniels (Princess Henriette), Lowell Sherman (King of France), Lois Wilson (Queen of France) Doris Kenyon (Lady Mary) Ian MacLaren (Duke of Winterset) (Leading Players). Adapted from Booth Tarkington's novel *Monsieur Beaucaire* (1900).

A Sainted Devil, Famous Players-Lasky, Paramount: 8,633 feet, premièred 15 November 1924. Joseph Henabery (Director); Forrest Halsey (Adapter); Harry Fischbeck (Photographer); Rudolph Valentino (Don Alonzo de Castro), Nita Naldi (Carlotta), Helen D'Algy (Julietta Valdez), Dagmar Godowsky (Doña Florencia) (Leading Players). Based on Rex Beach's story 'Rope's End', published in *Cosmopolitan*, May 1913.

Cobra, Ritz Carlton Productions, Paramount: 6,895 feet, premièred 30 November, 1925. Joseph Henabery (Director); Anthony Coldeways (Screenwriter); J. D. Jennings, Harry Fischbeck (Photographers); William Cameron Menzies (Set Designer); Gilbert Adrian (Dress Designer); Rudolph Valentino (Count Torriani), Nita Naldi (Elise van Zile), Casson Ferguson (Jack Dorning), Gertrude Olmstead (Mary Drake) (Leading Players). Adapted from Martin Brown's play *Cobra* (1924).

The Eagle, United Artists: 6,755 feet, premièred 8 November 1925. Clarence Brown (Director); Hans Kraly (Screenwriter); George Barnes, Dev Jennings (Photographers); George Marion Jr (Titles); Hal C. Kern (Editor); William Cameron Menzies (Art Director); Adrian (Dress Designer); Rudolph Valentino (Vladimir Dubrovsky), Vilma Banky (Mascha Troekouroff), Louise Dresser (Czarina), Albert Conti (Kuschka) (Leading Players). Adapted from Pushkin's novel *Dubrovsky* (1894).

Son of the Sheik, United Artists: 6,688 feet, premièred 9 July 1926. George Fitzmaurice (Director); George Barnes (Photographer); George Marion Jr (Titles); Frances Marion, Fred de Gresac (Adapters); Hal C. Kern (Editor); William Cameron Menzies (Art Director); Rudolph Valentino (Ahmed/The Sheik), Vilma Banky (Yasmin), George Fawcett (Andre), Agnes Ayres (Diana), Montague Love (Gabah, the Moor); (Leading Players). Adapted from Edith Maude Hull's novel *Sons of the Sheik* (1925).

Select bibliography

Arnold, Alan, *Valentino*, Hutchinson, 1952

Mackenzie, Norman A., *The Magic of Rudolph Valentino*, Research Publishing Co., 1974

Rambova, Natacha, *Rudy, An Intimate Portrait*, Hutchinson, 1926

Shulman, Irving, *Valentino*, Trident Press, 1967

Ullman, S. George, *Valentino As I Knew Him*, A. L. Burt, 1927

Index